APR 05 – July 05 = 3

 W9-ASC-467

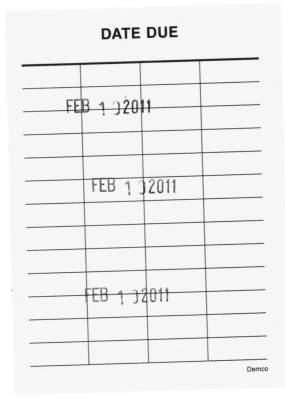

8/8

IT'S HER WEDDING
but
I'LL CRY IF I WANT TO

A SURVIVAL GUIDE
FOR THE MOTHER OF THE BRIDE

Leslie Milk

RODALE

© 2005 by Leslie Milk

Printed in the United States of America
Rodale Inc. makes every effort to use acid-free ⊖, recycled paper ♻.

Book design by Tara Long
Illustrations by Lisa Ballard

Library of Congress Cataloging-in-Publication Data

Milk, Leslie.
    It's her wedding, but I'll cry if I want to : a survival guide for the mother of the bride / Leslie Milk.
        p.   cm.
    ISBN-13 978–1–59486–001–0 hardcover
    ISBN-10 1–59486–001–7 hardcover
    1. Weddings—Humor.   I. Title: It is her wedding, but I will cry if I want to.   II. Title.
PN6231.W37M55   2005
392.5'02'07—dc22   2004019883

Distributed to the trade by Holtzbrinck Publishers

2   4   6   8   10   9   7   5   3   1   hardcover

We inspire and enable people to improve their lives and the world around them
For more of our products visit **rodalestore.com** or call 800-848-4735

FOR MEREDITH

The most beautiful bride ever to walk down the aisle.
And I'm not just saying that because I'm her mother.

Contents

Part 4

THE WEDDING POMP AND PROTOCOL

Part 5

THE WEDDING

Acknowledgments

Producing a book is a lot like producing a wedding—one person cannot do it alone. Neither of these enterprises started out as my idea. The bride and groom decided to get married without any prompting from me. It was my wise and witty husband, Benjamin, who suggested that I should document the experience and stalwartly lived through the 16 months of planning and another year of writing.

I am also very grateful to:

Jeremy, my fantastic son and sometime collaborator, who never once asked, "Why are you spending my inheritance on my sister's wedding?"

Susan Taylor, my best friend since the Brownies, who conveniently arranged to marry off both her children so that I would have more material.

The professionals who became my wedding professors: florist Nick Perez, photographer Michael Kress, and Cynthia Charles Andrade of Catering by Windows.

Jack Limpert, editor of *Washingtonian* magazine, for rationing my adjectives and making me a better listener as well as a better writer.

Mariska van Aalst, my book editor, the perfect combination of cheerleader, confessor, and thoughtful critic.

Jane Dystel, my literary agent, whose guidance and encouragement were invaluable.

Finally, I owe an enormous debt of gratitude to all of the brides and mothers of brides who shared their wedding stories with me.

May they all live happily ever after.

Part 1

THE WEDDING PARTY

1

THERE GOES MY BABY

Oh, my God, she's engaged!"

You shouldn't really be shocked by the news. She may not live at home or even in her hometown, but you've seen the signs.

First his name started cropping up in conversations. Then she was starting sentences with "Tim thinks" or "Josh and I."

After a suitable interval, you met the guy. Assuming your daughter is over the age of consent, you realized what this "meeting" meant. This guy was a contender. If he walked upright, his eyes focused, and he wasn't on a day pass from a nearby correctional facility, he was a serious contender.

You tried hard not to turn that initial encounter into a job interview. You only asked subtle questions like "Have you always lived with your mother?" Or "I've always wondered about the earning potential of periodontists. Will dental floss hurt your business in the long run?" You kicked your husband under the table before he could ask to see the guy's last three tax returns.

Then you waited to see if the guy moved up through the ranks:

A great guy

A guy I'm seeing

- The guy I'm seeing
- You called your daughter and he answered.
- You called your daughter and left a message on her answering machine although you knew she was spending weekends at his place and she knew that you knew, but neither of you was ready to acknowledge the knowledge.

They broke up and made up several times. She was invited to his sister's wedding. His mother bought her a birthday present. Still, you knew better than to get too excited. The average girl discovers boys at age 13. The average first-time bride is 25. That's more than a decade of possibles, impossibles, interims, and also-rans.

Then, one evening she called, and "Oh my God, she's engaged."

Your daughter will ask, "Are you happy?" This is a test. It is not multiple choice. You are ecstatic, overjoyed. Any tears you shed are tears of joy. The marriage may not last, but your daughter's memory of your response will live in infamy. And she's bound to tell the fiancé what you said!

Of course, you want to be happy for your daughter. But don't be surprised if you have mixed feelings. Her intended is a terrific guy . . . but he may not be the terrific guy you hoped for. When you pictured your daughter walking down the aisle, you probably expected her to marry someone close to home who shared your cultural and religious roots. You may even have unconsciously created a resume for the man of her dreams.

"I always thought she'd marry a doctor or a lawyer," one mother of the bride admitted. When it was pointed out to her that nobody in the bride's family was a doctor or a lawyer, she sighed, "I know that. But I always thought she'd marry up."

Even if the fiancé is everything you would wish for, this is as much a rite of passage for you as it is for her. I know how I felt when my daughter, Meredith, called with the news that she was engaged on Valentine's Day 2002. I really was ecstatic, overjoyed, weeping tears of joy. But after I hung up the phone, I suddenly felt . . . old.

Mother of the bride—the phrase conjures up a vision of a middle-aged woman with the kind of hairdo that doesn't move in a high wind. The mother of the bride wears a pastel jacket dress to hide her flabby upper arms and matching shoes with arch supports. She carries a purse big enough for her reading glasses. She asks the caterer for decaf. Nobody ever refers to the mother of the bride as "such a pretty girl."

I didn't want to see myself that way, but if the arch supports fit . . .

Like many other mothers of brides—and grooms—the first thing I asked was when the happy couple wanted to get married. The question had nothing to do with planning the ceremony, hiring the caterer, booking the hall, and so on. I needed to know how much time I had to get in shape for the wedding pictures. How much time I had would determine how many chins I would be wearing on the big day.

Would the engagement last long enough for a diet and rigorous workouts, or was I heading straight for Lycra, liposuction, and the "instant face-lift" with rubber bands and tape advertised on a late-night infomercial? How many hairdos and hair colors could I try before settling on the camera-ready coiffure?

Then I did something really dangerous—I pulled out my wedding album.

It is only natural to harken back to your own wedding or weddings when you think about your daughter as a bride. Hopefully, all your memories are happy ones. But if the glorious celebration was followed by a less-than-glorious marriage, if your blood pressure rises when you think of your young, innocent self walking down the aisle toward that idiotic, lowlife, no-good, cheating son of a fishwife, your recollections of the wedding itself may be colored by subsequent events.

That trip down memory lane is a voyage best taken alone. It is unfair to burden the bride with your romantic baggage. And if that idiotic, lowlife, no-good cheating son of a fishwife also happens to be the bride's father, you'll have to bite your tongue a lot in the months ahead. Nothing ruins a wedding faster than acrimonious exes using the event as an excuse to snipe at each other.

Happily married mothers face a different challenge. You may be tempted to re-create the magic. Depending on when you were wed and where your head was at the time, you probably had either a strictly traditional wedding, a love-in, a ceremony that didn't compromise your feminist principles, an earth-friendly affair with invitations on recycled paper, or some combination of all four.

A traditional wedding meant a white wedding gown with enough fabric to cover all of your admirable assets, a veil over your face, bridesmaids in matching pastel dresses, a white wedding cake, "Here Comes the Bride," and a vow to "love, honor, and obey."

The alternative wedding had readings from *The Prophet,* by Kahlil Gibran, a Mexican wedding dress, a barefoot-on-a-hillside ceremony, somebody playing the guitar, and a promise "to make love, not war." There was no wedding cake and nobody asked what was in the brownies.

Your feminist wedding may have skipped all mentions of bride and groom. You read from the gospel according to Gloria Steinem, you pledged to be equal partners, and neither of you changed your name.

Your "friends of the earth" wedding meant an unbleached cotton wedding dress, organic vegetables, and recycling bins at the reception.

Forget it!

Your daughter doesn't want the wedding you had. She has never read *Jonathan Livingston Seagull*. She would no more promise to "obey" than she would promise to churn butter. On the other hand, she may be more traditional than you were at her age, eager to embrace all of the rituals you thought were sexist and archaic.

As a young bride, you wouldn't have dreamed of marrying far from home. Today's engaged couples are likely to be from different geographic areas. Now that women marry later and venture farther, "home" for the bride and groom may be in another city. The couple may want to marry in another location altogether—a dream destination on an island, atop a mountain, in an amusement park, or in the adult version of an amusement park, Las Vegas.

As a bride, you wanted the best wedding your father's money could buy. Your daughter may want no part of an expensive shindig. Her style may be more funky than formal. As long as they don't pose a serious risk to life, limb, or bank balance, be prepared to honor the bride's choices.

In my case, this was not a problem. I wouldn't wish my one and only wedding on any other unsuspecting bride, let alone my darling daughter.

My husband, Benjamin, and I were married at the Plaza Hotel in New York on March 24, 1968. We are still married. I attribute some of our marital longevity to the fact that our wedding was such a disaster that the marriage had nowhere to go but up.

What went wrong? The hotel was not ravaged by flood or fire. The kitchen did not explode. My dress arrived on time and intact. We suffered none of the misfortunes that make great stories or are now covered by wedding insurance. Our problems were all human error: in-laws turning into outlaws, guests and hosts behaving badly, and the bride taking umbrage when she should have been taking valium.

My father-in-law hijacked the wedding. We were supposed to be married at a lovely little New York hotel overlooking Central Park. My father-in-law took it upon himself to inspect the site and announced that no son of his would be married there. He hated the men's room. He did not feel the need to list his specific complaints. He just turned purple at the mere mention of the place. (Let me hasten to point out that his other son had been married a few months earlier at a wedding mill famous for such special effects as having the bride appear on an elevated platform above the congregation amid a flock of doves and singing angels.)

Every time my future father-in-law turned aubergine, my mother-in-law took to her bed. After a month of this, we moved the wedding to the Plaza Hotel, which had well-appointed men's rooms that met my future father-in-law's standards.

My mother was so offended by the cavalier attitude of the groom's family, who were not paying for any part of the wedding, that she refused to speak to them or me. (She did deign to address me briefly before the ceremony to ask me to put on her false eyelashes.)

The Plaza gave us a "bridal suite" to dress for the wedding and for the wedding night. I was so thrilled—the suite was bigger than our first apartment—that I never asked how I would get from the suite to the wedding ceremony. There I was in my dress and veil, sharing the elevator with a couple from Indiana, a bellhop, and a luggage cart. The wife was very understanding. "Fred, don't step on her dress," she warned her husband. Then she wished me good luck.

☞ Many of my relatives had never met the groom. As he and the best man came down the aisle, my father's deaf Aunt Mollie could be heard "whispering," "Is he the fat one or the skinny one?"

☞ My husband's cousin Reggie, an entrepreneur who founded the largest transvestite mail-order business in the United States, hadn't been invited to the wedding. He came anyway, representing his mother who had been invited but couldn't make it. Reggie showed up with a date. We were so grateful that he wasn't wearing any of his own wares that we did not object to the extra guest.

☞ My cousin Jeanie, dressed in black in deference to her recently failed marriage, displayed so much cleavage that one of the waiters almost set himself on fire with the cherries jubilee.

I could go on, but . . .

I had no desire to duplicate my nuptial disaster. I wanted my daughter to have the wedding I never had—a happy one.

Like most brides today, my daughter was older than I was on my trip down the aisle and less likely to bow to parental pressure. But I did want her to benefit from my mistakes:

☞ I forgot that you have to have a wedding with your own relatives. You may crave an elegant affair, but unless you hire the cast of *Four Weddings and a Funeral* to play your family, it isn't going to happen.

☞ Contrary to conventional wisdom, weddings do not bring out the best in people. Rites of passage stir the emotional pot, and old hurts and grievances rise to the surface.

⌒ I should have let my mother do more of it. I was determined that the wedding should reflect my personality, and the only way to achieve that was to do it all myself. Wrong. My mother had trained her whole life for just such an opportunity. She was used to giving orders. Having survived the Great Depression and my grandmother, she would not have been cowed by my in-laws, my relatives, or the catering director at the Plaza who refused my husband's one request—a chocolate wedding cake.

Of course, my mother wouldn't have been cowed by me either.

But my daughter, Meredith, had no such problem.

And hopefully, neither will yours. Some brides have told me that their mothers were frustrated—their mothers planned their weddings and now they have daughters who want to run their own shows. It can be hard to relinquish control—particularly if you are paying some or all of the bills.

"She told me that this was her wedding; I could have 'mine' in 20 or 30 years when my daughter gets married," said one bitter newlywed.

Big mistake! Unless your aim is to permanently alienate your daughter and miss meeting your future grandchildren, you want to work *with* your daughter, not walk over her.

In this area, I had a distinct advantage. Some are born with guilt, some achieve guilt, and some have guilt thrust upon them. I qualify on all three counts.

As a working mother and a charter member of the "We can have it all and do it all" generation, I still feel guilty about mistakes I made trying to juggle work and family. Guilt, coupled with the memories of my wedding, were enough motivation for me to put my daughter's wishes first.

My daughter—like yours—is a very independent woman. Couldn't she have pulled the wedding together without my help? Not easily. Contrary to some popular opinion, mothers of the bride are far from obsolete.

The bride may be finishing school or starting a career. She may live hundreds or thousands of miles from home. She can and should make all of the big decisions—she picked the groom and she should pick the dress, the location, the officiant, and the style of the wedding. But she will happily delegate many of the details. She has no burning need to type lists, lick envelopes, or schlep invitations to the post office.

Broken, blended, and unconventional families present unimagined challenges for your daughter. Planning the ceremony and the seating arrangements can give the bride a headache that will last well into the honeymoon—and create animosities that live on even longer.

Whether you are her mother or her surrogate mother (stepmom, aunt, etc.) and whether she knows it or not, the bride is going to need you. And you are going to need help.

This book is your survival guide.

Reality Check #1

10 REASONS WHY EVERY BRIDE NEEDS A MOTHER OR SURROGATE MOTHER

1. You are the only one willing to work unlimited hours doing such menial jobs as typing lists, licking envelopes, and picking up and delivering for no pay.

2. You are the only other person who really cares whether the swirls on the wedding cake match the embroidery on her dress or if the yellow flowers are more citron than buttercup.

3. You'll negotiate the budget with the father of the bride and take the heat when the bills arrive.

4. You'll come to the rescue when the recalcitrant caterer refuses to make the groom's favorite pigs-in-blankets for the reception.

5. You'll go with her to 54 shoe stores looking for the perfect white wedding shoes even though you know that no one will see them under the wedding dress.

6. You'll go with her to every dress fitting and assure her that she's going to be a beautiful bride even if she doesn't lose the last 5 pounds.

7. You'll get the bridal salon to alter the wedding dress at the last minute when she does lose the last 5 pounds.

8. You'll entertain his mother and all of your relatives.

9. Whenever the bride begins to panic, she'll feel free to yell at you, knowing that you won't hate her in the morning.

10. After the wedding, you are the only one who'll be willing to watch the wedding video 20 times in the first month, marveling with the bride about every delightful detail.

2

THE MOTHER-DAUGHTER
PRENUPTIAL AGREEMENT

The moment your daughter announces that she's getting married, you start playing catch-up. What's news to you is the culmination of a decade of daydreams for her. By the time you get over the shock, she is hip deep in bridal magazines. By the time you've called all the relatives, she is mentally debating the advantages of a sunset wedding on a Bali beach or asking the president if the White House is available on a Saturday in June.

It is tempting to sit back and enjoy the moment.

You and your daughter have been through so much together. Book reports and braces. Good grades and bad hair days. Shouting matches you'll always remember and boyfriends you'd rather forget. There were times when you wondered whether the bond between you had stretched to the breaking point. But now you are both adults, able to relate woman-to-woman.

In the weeks or months ahead, the mother-daughter bond will again be tested as the two of you juggle the needs and wishes of two families and an army of bridesmaids, groomsmen, caterers, cake bakers, dressmakers, florists, photographers, videographers, musicians, and calligraphers. There are even instances, albeit rare, when you will have to consider the wishes of the groom.

You've heard the horror stories of mothers and brides locked in battle over the wording of the invitation or the makeup of the wedding party. Right now that kind of conflict seems impossible. But the longer your daughter lingers over those magazines, the more unrealistic her unspoken expectations can become.

She is not alone. You are probably harboring some illusions of the kind of wedding your daughter wants. Think that your daughter, the soccer goalie-turned-litigator, isn't going to want to drape herself in floor-length Valenciennes lace? Think again! Wedding fantasies have nothing to do with the woman she appears to be.

You have to start with the premise that every American girl is born with unalienable rights to life, liberty, and a long white dress. Girls in other countries are demanding those same rights, regardless of their roots. In Japan, even Buddhist brides are often married in Christian church ceremonies, just so they can wear the long white dress.

This is the time to get real. You will do your best to create the dream wedding, but not the impossible dream wedding. The only way she's getting married in the White House is if you get elected president, and she probably doesn't want to wait that long. She can indeed be married on a beach in Tahiti as long as she is willing to limit the wedding to immediate family and any flush friends who can pay their own way over.

Your daughter may be entertaining any number of ideas to make her wedding unique—having a nautical wedding on a yacht, re-creating a fairy tale like Snow White or Alice in Wonderland, or transforming a banquet hall into a fantasy from

Arabian Nights complete with bedoin tents and belly dancers. You need to make clear that 90-year-old Aunt Nancy won't be able to come to the casbah and sit on a cushion and that the bridesmaids may balk at being dressed as the seven dwarfs.

You'll have to get real, too. Of course, it would be lovely if she wore your wedding dress, but what was "mod" in the '70s looks mad now.

It is easy to misunderstand each other when you think you are communicating clearly. Your idea of an "informal" wedding may be a garden party with flutes of champagne. She's picturing a beach barbecue with bottles of beer.

The best way to achieve a true meeting of the minds and an alignment between bride and bank account is to put it in writing. Before you view the first hotel ballroom or taste the first chevres on endive, sit down together to draw up a mother-daughter prenuptial agreement. Putting it in writing can prevent the "she said, she said" misunderstandings that ruin many a wedding long before the "I dos."

It will force both of you to come up with a workable schedule. It is also a diplomatic way of asking the questions that need to be asked, like, "Is his family footing the bill for any part of this extravaganza or should I tell your father what this is going to cost us and hope he doesn't have a stroke?"

A mother-daughter agreement is a form of wedding insurance. In the unlikely event that the bride becomes a bridezilla (a technical term for "the bride from hell") or you turn into the Mother of all mothers of the bride, there will be clearly outlined procedures for intervention.

You don't need a lawyer to create a mother-daughter prenup. The following sample agreement can be modified to cover the specifics of your situation.

MOTHER-DAUGHTER PRENUPTIAL AGREEMENT

We the undersigned, _____, bride, and _____, mother of the bride, in order to preserve our relationship and our sanity and to create a more perfect wedding, agree to the following obligations and conditions:

Financial Arrangement: The cost of the wedding will not exceed $_____. The bride's family, the groom's family, and the bride and groom will divide the costs of the rehearsal dinner, wedding ceremony, reception, and honeymoon in the following way:
The bride and groom will pay for _____
The bride's family will pay for _____
The groom's family will pay for _____

Delineation of Responsibility: This is the bride's day to shine. She will have ultimate authority on the selection of the location, attire, and specific details of the wedding ceremony and reception, within the parameters of this agreement.

Wedding Style: The bride and groom have decided that the wedding will be:

__ **Formal**—black tie and seated dinner

__ **Semiformal**—black tie or dark suit and dinner or buffet

__ **Texas Formal**—black tie and boots, champagne and barbecue

__ **Informal**—shirts and shoes required

Wedding Theme: The bride is entitled to select a theme for the wedding. However, the mother of the bride is not required to wear a costume consistent with that theme.

Determination of the Guest List: The wedding will be limited to _____ guests to be divided in the following way:

Bride and groom _____

Bride's family _____

Groom's family _____

We recognize that if we invite everyone we know, love, like, associate with on a regular basis, or associate with on an irregular basis, we will have to rent the nearest football stadium, convention center, or high school gym. Since this is not the ambience we have in mind, we agree to cut down our guest lists to stay with the budget and the confines of our wedding venue in the following manner:

The mother of the bride agrees to eliminate all relatives she could not recognize on sight, friends and colleagues who wouldn't recognize the bride on sight, and anyone she would invite only because she owes them a dinner.

The bride agrees to eliminate old boyfriends invited for the express purpose of watching them suffer once they see how gorgeous she is now. She will also cross off high school chums and college sorority sisters she hasn't seen in the last five years, people at work she doesn't like but feels funny not inviting, and her entire kickboxing class.

Single friends of the mother of the bride will be invited to bring fiancées, partners, or romantic interests who have been around for at least three weeks prior to the making of the final guest list.

Single friends of the bride will be invited with fiancés, partners, boyfriends, potential boyfriends, or any male in a suit if any of the friend's old boyfriends are going to be present or if all of the ushers and friends of the groom are bringing wives, fiancées, or girlfriends.

The groom and his family are entitled to an equitable number of guests, regardless of the puny size of their family, the small number of friends you are certain they have, and their paltry financial contribution.

Maintenance of Civility: Both parties will refrain from using the following words or phrases during the planning process: tacky, tasteless, cutesy, cheesy, ugly, and atrocious. The mother of the bride will refrain from using the following phrases: "I wouldn't be caught dead in" "over my dead body" "I'm paying for it, so . . ." and "your (grandmother, grandfather, aunt, uncle) must be turning over in his/her grave" as well as all criticism of the groom and the groom's family—at least when talking to her daughter. (See Stipulated Bitching Hours clause.) The bride will refrain from using the following phrases: "Everybody else has . . ." "In the dark ages, when you were a bride . . ." and "If you really want me to be happy . . ."

Selection of the Officiant: The mother of the bride agrees that, guilt aside, the bride is under no obligation to be married in the faith of her forefathers. The bride agrees that she will select an officiant who is licensed to perform a legal marriage and is not a practitioner of Wicca, Raelianism, Scientology, occult worship, or satanism. Clergy ordained via the Internet or by mail order are acceptable as long as their eyes focus and they do not address the father of the bride as "Yo" or "Dude."

Selection of Location: The bride is not required to be married in the house of worship favored by her forefathers. She may select a romantic, elegant, or exotic location with the following exceptions:

If the location is outdoors, there must be a place to take cover in case of rain, snow, gale, or hurricane.

The families of the bride and groom should not need athletic ability or special inoculations to get there.

No location should be considered where the mother of the bride is required to wear a bikini or her birthday suit.

Selection of Attire: The bride agrees to consider but is under no obligation to wear a dress, veil, headpiece, garter, or any other article of wedding attire worn by mother, grandmother, or other relatives. The bride may select her own dress and accessories for the wedding, within the constraints of the budget.

The mother of the bride may select her own dress and accessories for the wedding with the understanding that she will not outshine the bride and not clash with the bride's color scheme. Her ensemble may be a bit more expensive than the bride's, but she's earned the right.

The mother of the bride will be responsible for assuring that male members of the bride's family are properly attired. In the case of a formal wedding, proper attire will constitute suits or tuxedos of recent vintage, formal shirts, and black shoes without lug soles.

Selection of Theme: The bride and groom may decide to select a theme for their wedding to reflect a shared interest, e.g., skydiving, skiing, or scuba diving; a shared passion, e.g., Star Wars or bridge; or their shared offbeat sense of humor, e.g., "Let's dress the wedding party like the cast of *Lion King*." The mother of the bride must defer to their wishes even though she has the old-fashioned notion that getting married is, in itself, enough of a theme to inspire a wedding.

However, the mother of the bride retains the rights stipulated in the location clause. In addition, she may elect not to come in costume, even if that means The Force will not be with her.

Drop-Dead Dates: If the bride has not found the "perfect" dress, veil, shoes, location, caterer, photographer, florist, or officiant 90 days before the date of the wedding, she is required to pick the best available.

Stipulated Bitching Hours: The mother of the bride agrees to grant the bride ____ hours to bitch without interruption about the groom, his unreasonable family, her unfeeling friends, her boss, her body, her hair, her skin, and the mother of the bride herself. The bride is under no obligation to reciprocate. However, the mother of the bride is entitled to equal time to bitch to her best friend about the groom, his unreasonable family, her boss, her body, her hair, her skin, and her unfeeling daughter.

The best friend will, of course, be sworn to secrecy and promise to forget all she has heard within 30 days after the wedding.

Assumption of Blame: The mother of the bride shall be held blameless for bad weather, bad hair days, bad karma, zits, and other acts of God. The mother of the bride agrees to be blamed for everything else—after all, what's a mother for?

Insanity Clause: Should either party to this agreement show signs of wedding madness, the father of the bride, the groom, and the maid of honor together may perform an intervention, requiring the bride or the mother of the bride to cease and desist all wedding-related activity for 24 hours. An exception will be made should this 24-hour period include the actual wedding day. Symptoms of wedding madness may include but are not limited to:

  Incoherent muttering of nonsense phrases like "arugula or radicchio, anemones or sweet peas, ivory or ecru."

  Requiring all of the attendants to dye their hair to match the bridal bouquet.

  Refusing to allow the groom's sister to be in the wedding unless she loses weight.

  Trying to hire the carriage that Princess Diana used to get to Westminster Abbey.

  Trying to steal another bride's photographer, florist, or videographer.

One Wedding Clause: The mother of the bride is thrilled that the bride has found her soul mate, the person she will love and cherish until death do them part. However, in the unlikely event that the bride does not find eternal bliss, it is understood that the family of the bride will underwrite one wedding and one wedding only. After that, honey, you're on your own.

Reality Check #2

10 THINGS A MOTHER SHOULD NEVER DISCUSS WITH THE BRIDE

1. What it really is (was) like to be married to her father

2. Her sex life—unless you are hoping to learn something

3. Your sex life—unless you are hoping to learn something

4. Any sentence that begins with "Marriage is . . ."

5. The ex-boyfriend you hoped she'd marry

6. The ex-boyfriend she hoped she'd marry

7. The ex-boyfriend you are glad she didn't marry

8. The groom's hair, clothes, career, friends, or how much time he spends watching sports

9. Whether the newlyweds will be coming to your house for Thanksgiving, Christmas, or Mother's Day

10. How soon you are going to be a grand-mother

FATHER OF THE BRIDE

The narrator in Thornton Wilder's *Our Town* said it best: "A man looks pretty small at a wedding, George. All those good women standing shoulder to shoulder, making sure that the knot's tied in a mighty public way."

Men don't know quite what to make of weddings. Weddings are to men what football is to women—we can understand the theory, we can appreciate the spectacle, we can admire the effort, but we just don't get the point. Why would anyone willingly invest so much time and trouble to engage in such a torturous activity? What's with the ridiculous outfits? Who made all the weird rules?

The language of football is as foreign to us as Aramaic. If it's a "Hail Mary" pass, why aren't they are on their knees?

The language of weddings is just as foreign to men. The father of the bride doesn't know what a "bustier" is, but it doesn't sound like something he wants his daughter wearing. Why would she want a chapel veil if she isn't becoming a nun? "Fondant" sounds like an agreement between warring nations. He has never worn a "freesia" in his life and he isn't about to start now.

Men would rather play and watch football without us. We'd rather organize weddings without them. Only in the company of our own kind can we cheer, scream, curse, dance around, and genuinely indulge ourselves in the sheer joy of our sport.

What adds insult to injury for the father of the bride is that he not only has to play the game—in many cases, he also has to pay for it.

It is cruel to add further insult by fostering the impression that the father of the bride has a major role in the planning or execution of the wedding. In truth, the father of the bride is like the corpse at the funeral—he has to be there, but no one expects him to do anything.

Some mothers point out that, while they do all the work, the wedding day itself turns into Father's Day. He gets the star turns—walking the bride down the aisle and dancing with his daughter in the spotlight.

It is a day when a father's absence is deeply felt. However, one could also argue that, if the father of the bride doesn't deign to show up, any guy in a dark suit will do. Now that independent brides feel free to walk themselves down the aisle, you can even skip the guy and the dark suit.

We have heard of cases where the fathers did want to play a major role in the planning. (We note a strong correlation between men who want to help plan weddings and men who hate football.) Even in these rare cases, said fathers did not want to get involved to the point of actual work. They saw themselves in an executive capacity, approving or vetoing choices once the mother and the bride had done all of the legwork, assembled all of the information, and narrowed down the possibilities. Or they went online to find a whole new set of possibilities that the women should investigate.

Some fathers negotiate the contracts with

vendors. If they do, make sure to stress that the object is not only to get the best deal but also to get the best service at the wedding itself. A happy florist or caterer is more likely to give their all to the bride.

The more Type A the father is, the less likely he is to type anything. You need help like this like you need a few new gray hairs. That is why it is wise to discourage the father of the bride at all costs.

Prior to the wedding itself, the father of the bride has a few ceremonial duties. First, he will often be called upon to take part in a very old ritual that is new again. The prospective groom may call or call upon the bride's parents and request their daughter's hand in marriage.

This is a rhetorical question. It is incumbent on the mother of the bride to make sure the father of the bride understands this.

She must also keep a straight face during the "asking for her hand" ritual. Being privy to more of our daughters' secrets than we are comfortable knowing, we are well aware that by this time, the groom has had her hand, her heart, and several other strategic parts. But snicker not! It is sweet of the groom to declare his intentions to make your daughter happy.

Up until now, the father of the bride hasn't focused on the man in his little girl's life or, for that matter, the last six men who lasted long enough to be introduced to the parents. After a while, all of his daughter's boyfriends blended together. "Was that the psych major, the mumbler, the musician, or the guy still trying to find himself but not looking on a regular basis?" the father will ask.

Over the years, he learned not to get too attached to previous boyfriends. By the time he learned their names, his daughter wanted to forget them.

Hopefully, the mother of the bride will get a heads-up about the hand request so that she can warn her husband.

Few fathers are prepared for the onslaught of activity that follows. First, his daughter calls to announce that—surprise, surprise—she's getting married. Before the father of the bride gets used to the idea of a son-in-law, he is being embraced, literally and figuratively, by a host of new relatives.

Wait a few days before you tell him that he's going to have to buy a new suit.

When Henry David Thoreau warned, "Beware of all enterprises that require new clothes," he was thinking like a father of the bride. Unlike the women in his life, the father of the bride may not see the need to purchase new finery for the wedding. If he owns a tuxedo or a dark suit, he is fully prepared to wear it on the big day. That may not be such a good idea. My husband had planned to wear the tuxedo he had worn for

35 years, even though the jacket buttoned only for the first 10.

Even if the suit fits, it may not fit the occasion. The groom sets the sartorial tone. He may choose to go casual in a light suit or a blazer and khakis for an informal summer wedding. He may opt for a modern look—tuxedo with a vest and straight tie instead of a bow tie. Grooms often wear embroidered white shirts called guayaberas for weddings in Mexico or Puerto Rico. Grooms in Hawaii show up in flowered shirts and garlands of leaves. The father of the bride does not have to match the groom exactly, but he should match his degree of formality.

When actor Russell Crowe got married, he wore a knee-length frock coat designed for him by Giorgio Armani. I cannot imagine a father of the bride carrying that look off without looking like an extra from a B movie.

If the groom chooses to emulate his Scottish ancestors and wear a kilt, his groomsmen may be obligated to expose their knees in similar fashion. However, if the father of the bride is not built for a kilt, he can be spared the embarrassment. He can wear a traditional suit.

Sometimes the groom's sartorial flight of fancy will be welcomed by the father of the bride. A couple who chose to re-create a renaissance wedding found the father of the bride eager to pull out an old brocade vest and boots he had worn in his hippie youth. They still fit and definitely fit the occasion.

The father of the bride should also be prepared for the traditional dance with his daughter during the reception. He may want to practice in advance or even take lessons (see Chapter 27). Nobody expects him to be John Travolta, and your daughter will be mortified if he tries to be. They may just shuffle back and forth to a slow song.

However, a little practice will keep him off her feet and her dress.

As the wedding host, the father of the bride often says a few words of welcome at the wedding itself. Encourage him to practice this, too. Hoping for inspiration at such an emotional moment can be risky—and every flub will be captured for posterity on video.

Benjamin began his speech by stating that, "For the past 16 months, I have felt like the invisible man." That wasn't entirely true. We took him and the groom to see the venue before we booked it. He had a say in the guest list, the wording of the invitation, and the seating plan. We invited him to the tasting with the caterer. We asked him to decide whether we should have a trio or a quartet playing at the ceremony, and he picked the instruments.

Another mother of the bride had an even better approach. She gave her husband one absolute veto—as long as it wasn't the groom. He nixed the Wedding March.

I spared Benjamin much of the maddening minutia that staging a wedding entails.

I spared him something else, too—he never saw a single bill. Once we agreed on the amount we were willing to spend for the wedding, my daughter set the budget priorities and I signed the contracts and paid the bills. Benjamin never had to think about what it was costing to have a stretch limousine sitting outside empty for three hours waiting to whisk the bride and groom away or the price of each centerpiece or each bridesmaid's bouquet.

There is often one expenditure that seems so outrageous to the father of the bride that he is convinced that both the bride and her mother have lost their minds.

It may be the extra fee for chair covers with bows on the back—I'm with him on that one. It may be programs—"If the guests don't know who the bride and groom are, what are they doing at the wedding?" Other common complaints include:

"Why do we need both a photographer and a videographer?"

"If the wedding is in a garden, why do we need a florist?"

"Why do we need a limousine when we have a perfectly good car?"

There is no satisfactory answer to these questions. You can't justify these necessities any more than he can explain the critical need for the Dallas Cowboys cheerleaders.

In my own defense, not that I need one, I stayed within the agreed-upon budget—motivated in part by all of the smug fathers of the brides I knew who had joked, "I gave my wife an unlimited budget and she exceeded it." I did tell Benjamin about all the frequent-flier miles I was earning just for him whenever I paid with a credit card.

When it comes to subterfuge, my abilities pale beside other mothers of brides who shared their strategies for increasing their husbands' tolerance for wedding extravagance. Several women told me that they looked their husbands straight in the eyes and said, "You tell your daughter that she can't have the (place, dress, bouquet, band) of her dreams."

One mother went so far as to agree with her husband that the designer dress her daughter loved was out of the question. "It's just too much. She'll only wear it once," the mother said as their daughter modeled the beautiful dress.

Even the bride-to-be told her doting dad that the gown was too expensive. Then she turned to go back into the dressing room to take off the fabulous creation.

In the end, the father of the bride insisted that they buy the dress, over the objections of both mother and daughter.

It is an insult to both men and women to imply that we can't manage money and that they are easily bamboozled by their wives. I prefer to think of my arrangement with Benjamin as a division of responsibility. He was in charge of his Red Zone and I was in charge of mine.

Reality Check #3

WHAT THE FATHER OF THE BRIDE SHOULDN'T SAY— EVEN IN JEST

1. Whew! We were afraid she'd never get married.

2. I guess the boob job was worth it.

3. The first time we met Adam, he looked like a drug dealer.

4. The first time we met Adam, we thought he was gay.

5. Adam is a prince compared to some of Becky's other boyfriends.

6. Becky and her MasterCard bill are all yours now, son.

7. This wedding cost me $50,000. That's $200 a plate, folks, so I hope you will give to these kids and give generously.

8. My new son-in-law needs a job. I have his resume right here.

9. Don't worry, son. Becky won't ever get old and gray. She already colors her hair and she can always have a face-lift—just like her mother.

THE GROOM WITH A VIEW

Now that couples marry later, the chances are that your daughter is marrying a man who has something your husband never had—a lifestyle. He hasn't been living in a fraternity house or the postcollege version of a fraternity house where home maintenance meant fumigation every six months whether it needed it or not. He may actually own matching furniture, more than one pot, and wall hangings that don't feature zoned-out rock stars or nubile maidens with staples in their navels.

In short, he is an adult. And he may not want to sit idly by while you plan one of the most important days of his life.

"Twenty or 30 years ago, the groom didn't want to step on anyone's toes," according to Mark Walerstein, founder of GroomsOnline.com. Now they want a piece of the planning action. And, since more of them are chipping in to pay for the festivities, they aren't afraid to have their say on what they're paying for.

The Wall Street Journal, hardly a publication aimed at a "moon, spoon, June" audience, recently covered the trend. The wedding industry, a $50 to $72 billion business, depending upon who's counting, has discovered men. Few men buy magazines with blushing brides on their covers, but future grooms are checking out online wedding sites. Web sites are now adopting "just us guys" features. On theknot.com, grooms are greeted with, "Congratulations, buddy, you finally got up the nerve to pop the big one."

One sign of this new interest is that grooms aren't content to pop the question in an ordinary way. They are creating elaborate proposal scenarios. In my hometown, Washington, D.C., there is even a proposal consultant to help grooms plan their big moment. There is such a premium on romantic proposals that the Learning Channel has an entire show devoted to them. It is almost as if proposing has become a competitive sport with extra points for ingenuity and the difficulty of the maneuver.

One man who met his future wife in elementary school took her back to the scene of the crime. He made arrangements with a custodian to have the school open after hours so he could propose there. An Atlanta romantic proposed in the ice cream parlor where the couple had their first date. He had arranged for an ice cream flavor to be named for his future bride.

But they are amateurs compared to the prospective groom who arranged for a friend to spirit his lady love to the Central Park boathouse on a pretense. The bride-to-be was sweaty and still in jogging clothes after an 18-mile training run before the New York Marathon. The next thing she knew, she was being blindfolded and shoved into a boat. When she removed her blindfold, the gullible girl was in the middle of a lake, in a boat with her boyfriend and a lot of roses. He presented her with a three-diamond engagement ring and a banana to replenish her potassium level.

Then there was the groom who buried the ring on the beach and couldn't find it again. The story has a happy ending, thanks to the Shelter Island police force and a few metal detectors.

My son-in-law devised a complicated scavenger hunt for the ring. He invited Meredith to dinner and told her to follow clues scattered throughout his house—the house he shared with his brother and their two dogs. What could be more romantic than scrounging through dirty socks under the bed or blindly reaching behind sofa cushions, hoping you don't find something moldy or worse?

At least he didn't hide the ring in her dessert or drop it into her drink, as other grooms have done. Imagine ingesting your engagement ring and then waiting to retrieve it!

Humorist Dave Barry recently wrote that "the groom's sole responsibility is to arrive at the ceremony wearing pants and not actively throwing up." Barry is way behind the times. Guys who invest so much in the preliminaries aren't about to be shut out of the main event.

Nearly 80 percent of brides report that their fiancés are interested in planning the wedding, according to the Fairchild Bridal Infobank. Both *Bride's* and *Modern Bride* magazines now include wedding checklists for grooms that reflect their increased involvement in the planning process. So don't be surprised if your daughter's intended starts humming "Here Comes the Groom" and laying out his likes and dislikes.

My daughter's fiancé, Tony, made only a few requests:

- A wedding on a three-day weekend or a Saturday night so his friends wouldn't have to go to work the next day

- A guest list large enough to include all of his friends

- Food he recognized

Like the bride, the groom has probably been to plenty of weddings and amassed a mental inventory of likes and dislikes. These should be respected. Food and drink are major factors for grooms—particularly for men who have become good cooks or wine connoisseurs. The groom should attend the tasting before the wedding or, at the very least, have say in the final menu.

He should also be consulted about beverage service. He may well feel that only single malt is good enough for his buddies or that drinking beer from a glass is an unnatural act. Encourage him to express himself. Then you and the bride can do what you planned to do anyway.

You are actually doing the groom a great service. Think of this process as good practice for married life.

Grooms often have strong views about music, too. Tony walked down the aisle to a song by his favorite band, the Grateful Dead.

He also helped put together the playlist for the deejay. Couples often listen to tapes of bands or go to see them perform before hiring a group for their wedding. The music should reflect the wedding couple's tastes. But you can request that the band or the deejay have a broad enough repertoire that people of all ages can listen to, if not dance to, the music. You may need to remind the groom that although you respect his passion for rap, most of the guests still think that a "hood" is something you wear and a "ho" is a chuckle from Santa Claus.

Some grooms with business backgrounds may want to negotiate some of the vendor contracts. Some are very interested in writing their own vows. Some may even have preferences about flowers, invitations, and seating arrangements.

The *Journal* wrote about one man who designed a wedding program printed on rice paper with miniature pinwheels inside.

Each program was tied with raffia twine. He also created placecards that doubled as wind chimes. And he felt so strongly about the flowers that it was nearly roses and tulips at 20 paces. "It's my wedding, too," he said. "It has to have my flair as well."

This guy is still the exception. The typical groom will have used up most of his romantic energy on the proposal. He wants to have his say on the aspects of the wedding that matter to him, but he doesn't want to deal with the endless wedding minutia that fascinate you and the bride.

One part of the process that confounds many grooms is the addressing of the wedding invitations. Don't be surprised if his list contains guests with names like "Scooter," "Boz," "Bubba," or "Mac." When you ask for the real names of these compatriots, you may be met with a blank stare. He has no idea that Boz is Herbert Francis Bozwell Jr. There is a good reason for this. His buddy Boz has spent considerable effort keeping his given name a secret.

You can insist on blowing Boz's cover or you can address an invitation to Mr. and Mrs. Boz Bozwell. Personally, I'd save Herbert Francis from the horror of seeing his hated name on a great big envelope and on a placecard for all to see.

You never expected the groom to become an active partner in the planning. You envisioned mother-daughter bonding over every wedding detail. You'll still have plenty of opportunities for that—shopping for the dress and working out dozens of details the groom couldn't care less about. But you have to step back gracefully when the bride and groom decide to do some of the wedding planning by themselves.

Think of it as an opportunity to get to know your new son-in-law better. A wedding isn't a day—it's a process. Part of that process is learning to share your daughter with a husband and a new family. You are also developing your own relationship with your future son-in-law.

If you and your daughter are engaged in an ongoing battle of wills about the wedding, consider the possibility that she may have recruited the groom to fight on her side. Many a protective groom feels the need to confront the woman who is making his future wife cry.

It is unlikely that the groom will turn into Groomzilla, so obsessed by wedding details that he drives even the bride crazy. But it does happen. One groom vetoed the bride's hometown as a wedding venue and changed the orders for the wedding cake and the invitations after the bride had ordered them. He wouldn't let anyone drink at the rehearsal dinner so there would be no hungover attendants at the wedding. He continually bugged the bride to exercise so she would be able to fit into her wedding dress.

Another budding P. T. Barnum arranged to arrive on an elephant. His bride had begged him to come in on a camel, which was cheaper to rent, but he refused. One Texas wedding planner dealt with a groom who called her six times a day and bemoaned the fact that the chair sashes at the reception were the wrong color.

Your son-in-law to be is probably looking better already!

What's more, he's probably working hard to look good at the wedding, too. More than 80 percent of grooms surveyed said they plan to whiten their teeth, and nearly 50 percent are working on their weight. Manicures, tanning sessions, and other beauty treatments are also becoming more popular.

So it is not surprising that grooms have definite ideas on what they want to wear to the wedding. The most popular options are:

- Traditional black tie: a tuxedo with a white shirt and a bow tie
- Updated black tie: a tuxedo and a pastel silk tie. Some grooms add a matching vest.
- Black suit worn with a pale solid-color shirt and a pastel silk tie
- Blue suit worn with a pale solid-color shirt and a solid-color or thin-striped tie
- Light-colored suit worn in the summer with a pale shirt and tie

Tony chose updated black tie. We were so pleased that he agreed to forego his customary baseball hat that we would have been happy if he wore a caftan and sandals—in basic black, of course.

Black suits and regular ties are rapidly gaining in popularity, since grooms don't want to struggle with bow ties and cummerbunds. Face it, a cummerbund is really a girdle worn outside the pants to create the illusion that a man's belly doesn't bulge out over his waistband. The chances are that the groom is young enough and fit enough so that he doesn't need a cummerbund to keep his paunch in upright position. If the father of the bride was counting on a cummerbund, he may be out of luck. Encourage him to start doing sit-ups, just in case.

Creative grooms may want to adopt variations on these themes from Celtic kilts to cowboy boots. Try not to comment on his knobby or chubby knees. As long as the bride is happy, you should be happy, too.

No, you can't tell him to take out his earring. But you can suggest that he change from a gold hoop to a diamond stud, in keeping with the formality of the occasion.

Reality Check #4

5 THINGS THE MOTHER OF THE BRIDE
SHOULD NEVER ASK THE GROOM

1. Are you sleeping with my daughter?

2. How much are your parents spending on the rehearsal dinner?

3. When are you getting rid of your old (couch, car, recliner, dog)?

4. Are you going to shave your (beard, mustache, head, back) before the wedding?

5. How soon am I going to be grandmother?

5

MEET THE PARENTS

A love story is a story of boy meets girl. The sequel, the wedding story, is a story of boy's parents meet girl's parents. And the sequel can have all of the twists and turns, low comedy, and high drama of the original.

As soon as your daughter gets engaged, she acquires a new family. They may seem like a group of strangers whose sole claim to fame is that they produced the prince among men who was wise enough to recognize your daughter's worth. But these strangers are going to be part of her life.

They are going to be part of your life, too. These people will share the wedding day, they will have dibs on your daughter for holidays and celebrations, and they will be forever tied to your grandchildren.

Considering the stakes, it pays to proceed with caution when you meet the in-laws for the first time. No matter how normal they appear, they are an unknown tribe with their own secret rituals, unspoken language, and ancient history that you and your daughter have no way of knowing. You have to prepare for the first meeting of the two families the way an anthropologist prepares to introduce herself into a native community.

- Do your homework to avoid taboos.

- Come bearing gifts.

- Be prepared for mixed signals.

- Try to remain open—or appear open—to whatever strange customs and rituals the natives practice.

- Use every opportunity to learn more about the members of the tribe—especially things your daughter never thought to tell you about the groom or he never thought to tell her.

- Don't expect to achieve intimacy overnight. (In fact, a little distance is healthy.)

- Remember that you may well be speaking different languages. Your "small" wedding may mean a mere 300 people to the other side. Your "immediate family" may mean kissin' cousins in seven states.

One Chicago mother of the bride was delighted to have the groom's family host the rehearsal dinner, until she learned that to them "rehearsal dinner" was just that. They would only invite the bridal party. If a bridesmaid had a husband, he was expected to fend for himself. In the end, the bride's family hosted the rehearsal dinner as well as the wedding. The groom's parents weren't wrong. Cheap, maybe, but not wrong. They were abiding by the rules of their tribe.

As soon as your daughter tells you that she is engaged, you'll want to call the groom's family. Do this right away, even though some etiquette experts suggest that they should call you. A surprise move gives you the upper hand in setting the time and place for your first meeting.

Start by introducing yourself—considering the limited communications abilities of many men, the groom's parents may have no idea that the bride-to-be is not an orphan.

After that, you should express your joy

about the engagement. Just be sure that you don't sound so happy that the parents begin to wonder whether you doubted that your daughter would ever land a live one.

If the groom's parents are divorced, whom do you call? Ask the bride. You may want to call both biological parents, starting with the parent he lived with last.

If the groom's family lives within driving distance, you should also make a date to get together. Be sure to include the bride and groom. After all, they are your common bond. If the groom's family lives out of town, tell them how much you are looking forward to meeting them before the wedding.

How soon should you meet the in-laws? Give yourself enough advance time to pump your daughter about the family. You need to ask about religion, politics, economic status, and membership in the DAR, GOP, NRA, NOW, AARP, and so on.

Are they teetotalers? Wine connoisseurs? Bourbon and branch drinkers? Do they entertain lavishly or not at all? Are they old-world formal or new-age casual?

You'll also want to Google them. (It doesn't hurt to Google the prospective son-in-law, too.)

What you learn will give you a feel for the kind of wedding they are likely to expect for their child.

There are limits, of course. I'm not suggesting that you hire a private investigator, check the father's credit rating, or attempt to obtain the parents' fingerprints for a criminal background check. There is plenty of time for that later!

The more research you do in advance, the less likely you are to be surprised at your first meeting. No matter how different the in-laws turn out to be, you can handle it with aplomb if you are prepared.

A few years ago, newspapers in several cities carried the announcement of the Detroit wedding of Elena Anne Ford to Joseph Daniel Rippolone. Readers learned that Ms. Ford worked for the family business—the Ford Motor Company. She was the daughter of automobile heiress Charlotte Ford and the late Stavros Niarchos, a Greek shipping tycoon.

The groom was identified as a plumber and mechanic who designs heating and plumbing systems. His parents were Angela and Robert Rippolone of Mastic Beach, Long Island. His mother worked as a telephone company representative. His father had retired as a bartender at Casa Basso, a restaurant in Westhampton.

The wedding had taken place in a chapel at the Henry Ford Museum in Dearborn, Michigan.

The Fords and the Rippolones may have been great buddies from way back. Maybe they had broken bread over broken pipes or whiled away many an evening at Casa Basso. But if they were strangers when they met, that first meeting would have been awkward if the bride had not briefed her mother on what to expect.

You'll also need to find out what your daughter has told the groom's family about you. We were well into the wedding planning before we learned that Meredith had assured her fiancé's family that we would pay for the whole wedding. They offered to pay for the rehearsal dinner and the morning-after brunch for out-of-towners. It worked out just fine, but it would have been nice to know what Meredith promised before she promised it.

You also need time to work on your mother-daughter prenup, so that you are clear on the kind of wedding she wants and she is clear on your funding limits.

However, you do want to talk to the groom's family before you commit to a wedding date. You don't want to hire the hall only to find out they have a major conflict. Of course, the groom should know this, but . . .

When you are ready to meet the parents, the location matters less than the duration of the initial meeting. Think of it like a first date—it should be more than coffee and less than a weekend. You'll start by expressing once again your delight that their son and your daughter have found each other.

You may be tempted to start talking about the wedding right away. Bite your tongue! Let your daughter lead any discussion about the wedding itself, indicating that you are deferring to the bride's and groom's wishes and you expect his family to follow suit.

His mother may have an heirloom wedding dress and no daughter to wear it, but you don't expect your daughter to wear your dress, let alone hers. Without being insulting, you can convey that you respect the couple's judgment and so should they.

The groom's mother may tell you that they have a large, close family, that every one of their other children got married in their neighborhood church, or that she hates Sunday afternoon affairs. You don't need to respond to these not-so-subtle hints. But you do want to hear them. All of this is good information to have. The more you know about the family dynamics, the easier it will be to understand how his family will react to wedding plans.

Could I have anticipated my father-in-law's men's room meltdown? (You recall, he freaked out about the facilities at a lovely hotel on Central Park South, forcing us to move the wedding to the Plaza.) Probably not. But I realize now that Benjamin's parents relied on Benjamin for so many things that our marriage must have been frightening for them. They couldn't have cared less about gaining a daughter. They were losing their oldest son.

Parental mixed feelings are a normal part of engagements. Don't be surprised if you bristle when the in-laws talk about how much they love your daughter and how they can't wait until she joins them for their annual Christmas skiing vacation in Aspen.

She's your kid and she should be home throwing tinsel on your Christmas tree, not gallivanting off to a ski slope with these strangers. Where were they when she had the chicken pox or failed an algebra test? Where were they during her mean teen years when she announced that instead of college she planned to attend "the school of life"?

Meanwhile, back at the wedding discussion, you hear your husband accepting the groom's family's offer to host the rehearsal dinner. That is your cue to end the evening before he commits you and the bride to anything else.

Many thirtysomething couples plan and pay for part or all of their own weddings, which makes the meeting of the two families largely ceremonial. Still, you'll want to support your daughter's decision to have the wedding of her choice.

In our community, parents who have the ability to pay for a wedding still foot the bills. But we've learned that there are no hard-and-fast rules about who pays for what.

In days of yore, the groom and his family paid for the rehearsal dinner, the bride's wedding ring, the bride's bouquet and going-away corsage, corsages for the mothers and grandmothers, all boutonnieres, the marriage license, the officiant's fee, and the honeymoon. You can still buy a set of "wedding responsibility cards" that outline these expectations in black and white. They may soon become collector's items.

Now everything is negotiable—but it is better if you don't do the negotiating. Let the groom talk to his family about what, if anything, they want to contribute to the wedding festivities.

Several fathers of brides I know did broach the subject of money with fathers of grooms, and the results were universally disastrous. The fathers of grooms seemed outraged at being asked, and the fathers of brides were outraged at their in-laws' outrage. In one case, the bride's family charged the groom's family a cost per head for their guests. The bride's father flirted with the idea of prorating the cost of the band, the officiant, and so on. The mother of the bride convinced him to drop that idea in the name of family unity.

Things got particularly testy when specific dollar amounts were mentioned. One groom's family said that they paid for their daughter's wedding and expected their son's intended's family to do likewise. Later the bride's family learned that the groom's father weaseled out of paying for that one, too.

Your best bet is to leave any discussions about money with the groom's family to the groom himself. If he wants to raise it, fine. If not, budget accordingly.

Sometimes the groom's family has much greater resources and expectations than the bride's parents do. You know that you have always done your best for your daughter, regardless of your bank balance. It makes no sense to go into debt to prove you can compete with the in-laws.

There are several ways to handle this situation—you can give your daughter the best wedding you can afford, you can split the costs with the in-laws, or you can graciously accept their offer to pay for the lion's share of the wedding.

If the bride and groom don't want an elaborate affair, you should accede to their wishes and suggest that the groom's family can host a big party for the couple at a later date. This is one of those times that having a mother comes in handy. If the bride is afraid to offend her future in-laws, she can blame it all on you!

Shouldn't the groom be able to tell his parents to back off? Yes, he should. If he cannot stand up to his parents, your daughter may question his commitment to their union. On the other hand, the prewedding period is a time of shifting allegiances and uncertain emotions. Your future son-in-law would not be the first groom to panic when he is caught in the crossfire between his mother and his fiancée. You can only stand back, support your daughter, and

wait for the dust to settle. Try not to point out how much more reasonable and accommodating you are than that other mother!

Splitting some or all of the costs of the wedding often makes sense. At one wedding, the bride's family planned to serve only wine and soft drinks. The groom's family wanted a full bar and offered to pay for it. Both families felt fine about the arrangement. In other cases, the groom's parents have paid to invite extra guests or to have more expensive flowers. One French family brought the champagne for the wedding, not trusting Americans to deliver the quality of bubbly they expected. The bride's family's reaction? "Vive la France!"

What if your daughter truly wants the expensive wedding that only her bridegroom's family can afford? For example, when the son of the owner of the Biltmore Hotel in Coral Gables, Florida, married the daughter of an Ohio pharmacist, the groom's family put the hotel and all of its staff at the couple's disposal for the wedding. The bride was eager to accept, and her family recognized the opportunity for what it was — a generous gesture and an opportunity to blow their wedding budget on something great for themselves.

Don't sell your daughter short. If she was raised with the right values, she isn't about to forget you just because her fiancé's family has more money. Even if she has the wrong values, think of the upgraded birthday and Christmas presents in your future.

Once the basic wedding plan is in place, you'll want to keep the groom's family apprised of the details. My daughter's future mother-in-law joked that it was her job to "shut up and wear beige." Had we taken her at her word, we would have missed an opportunity to strengthen family ties. We in-

vited her to the first wedding gown fitting, showed her the wedding venue, told her well in advance how many guests she could invite, and invited her to the tasting.

She was incredibly agreeable—almost too agreeable. She was overjoyed to be getting Meredith into the family. This made me wonder about Tony's previous girlfriends. Had he previously been involved with biker babes and bank robbers?

Many a family feud has erupted over the apportioning of guests at a wedding. Our mothers usually hogged the guest list, grudgingly allowing us a few friends (the ones they liked). The groom's family took whatever number of invitations they got and liked it.

When they didn't like it, they came to the wedding and glowered at the bride and her parents. Trust me, that is not an auspicious start to a marriage. I know something about glower power from my own wedding, and it isn't pretty.

That approach doesn't fly anymore. Most wedding lists are split three ways: one third for the bride's family, one third for the groom's family, and one third for the bride and groom together. We divided the guest list into quarters: one fourth for the bride's family, one fourth for the groom's family, one fourth for the bride, and one fourth for the groom.

This worked better in theory than in practice. One-quarter came out to 42.5 people. None of us were eager to fork over our half a person without a fight.

If the groom has more than one set of parents and a corresponding number of stepbrothers, half sisters, and "adopted" grandparents, frankly, that isn't your problem. The groom can sort this out with his complicated family. Let them glower at each other!

Many brides don't care whether the mothers wear dresses that match their color scheme, as long as they don't clash hideously with the wedding party. The groom's mother will often follow your lead, waiting to hear whether you are wearing a long dress or a short one and what color you have chosen. Try not to keep her in suspense. One mother of the bride, desperate to lose as much weight as she could before the big day, waited until the week of the wedding before she broke down and bought a dress. She was certain of only one thing, she told the mother of the groom—the dress wouldn't be black.

The groom's mother hedged her bets by buying two dresses but not taking the tags off until she heard from the bride's mother. She was biting her nails for weeks and finally had to make an executive decision to have one of the dresses altered. Both mothers looked lovely—the groom's mother in silver and the bride's mother in—you guessed it—black.

During the prewedding period, you'll confront some sensitive issues. You'll have to handle differences with diplomacy.

At one wedding, religious differences could have been an issue. The couple solved the problem by being married by a dentist who was "ordained" to officiate at marriage ceremonies. They were married in a hotel ballroom instead of a house of worship. The word "God" was never mentioned. The officiant did not impose his own theology either—he never once mentioned his 11th commandment, "Thou Shalt Floss after Every Meal."

At another wedding, both families were Jewish but only the groom's family was strictly observant. The bride's mother picked a menu that would not offend the groom's kosher family.

What if the groom's mother cannot contain her disapproval of the bride's wedding choices as "tacky," "tasteless," or "inappropriate"? You could remind her that one of the bride's major choices was her son.

Reality Check #5

KNOW THY IN-LAWS: A QUIZ FOR THE BRIDE

Your daughter may be so besotted with their son that she misses important clues. Ask these questions to get the picture.

1. Any photos with celebrities on display in their house? If so, were the parents pictured with:

    a. Bill Clinton
    b. Billy Graham
    c. Billy Joel
    d. Billy Idol

2. What was on the front lawn:

    a. A lamppost
    b. A pink flamingo
    c. A jockey statue
    d. A 1963 Ford

3. The groom's dad refers to the groom's mom as:

    a. Mother
    b. The old ball and chain
    c. My lovely wife
    d. That cow I used to be married to

4. The groom's mom refers to the groom's dad as:

    a. Father
    b. My idiot husband
    c. Mr. Wonderful
    d. That cheapskate I used to be married to

5. Dinner at his parents' house is:

    a. Filet mignon and foie gras
    b. Fried chicken and mashed potatoes
    c. Spaghetti served family style
    d. Pass the Doritos

7. When the groom turned 21, his parents gave him:

    a. Keys to a new car
    b. Microsoft stock
    c. A Bible
    d. The complete works of the Rolling Stones

8. The last time his family had a party it was:

    a. A catered dinner for 50
    b. A potluck book group discussion
    c. A tailgate before 'Bama beat Clemson
    d. Don't you need friends to give a party?

REVENGE OF THE BRIDESMAID

The first time a young woman is asked to be a bridesmaid, she is thrilled. The second time, she wants to be part of a special friend's wedding, but she reserves her excitement until after she sees the bridesmaid's dress. The sixth time, she loves her friend too much to decline, but the thought of buying another unflattering dress, flying across the country for every wedding-related event, buying shower and wedding presents, and hosting another bachelorette party may not fill her with unbridled joy. The eighth time . . . she just hopes there isn't another time.

A bridesmaid's dress is the only garment a woman will ever have to buy regardless of how much it costs or how it looks on her. To add insult to injury, she'll probably have to invest in alterations, accessories, and shoes to go with the unflattering dress. And smile while she does it.

Your daughter probably has a closet full of peach, cranberry, and ice blue creations, each with its own matching sash, stole, and shoes. She has shelled out a king's ransom in plane fares, hotel bills, engagement gifts, shower gifts, and wedding presents for her dearest friends. What kept her from stuffing the chiffon shawl up the bride's nose was the knowledge that her day would come.

Now it's payback time!

Some older brides are told that they should scale back their wedding parties because it is unseemly to have a gaggle of girls around you when you—and they—have passed the first flush of youth. The opposite is true. The older you are, the more women owe you.

There is no law that says that bridesmaids' dresses have to be ugly or unflattering. But the chances of finding a dress in a color and style that looks good on several women are slim. What's more, brides are subject to flights of fancy as they envision their wedding day. Don't be surprised if your daughter picks something for her wedding party to wear that is uncharacteristic. My daughter lives in jeans and T-shirts. She picked a tea-length, strapless dress with a sash for her attendants to wear. It was pink plaid. Her maid of honor and her bridesmaids—all eight of them—were young and slim and looked lovely in the dress. But it is unlikely that any of them will wear it again. A pink plaid dress with a sash is rarely the attire of choice for any girl over the age of 10.

In my daughter's defense, all brides seem to suffer from attacks of W.B. (wedding blindness), which affects their sense of color and proportion. They are unable to visualize a middle range, which explains the preponderance of dresses with huge skirts. Or they go to the other extreme. In my one outing as a bridesmaid, the dress was so tight that none of us could sit down in it—we had to kneel in the car on our way to the church.

Some brides choose to express their individuality with a wedding theme. It is only fair to tell the wedding party in advance if the theme will require bridesmaids and ushers to appear in costume. For example, a couple of Star Trek fanatics held their wedding in something akin to a Trekkie theme park, and the attendants wore Star Fleet uniforms.

A Maryland couple, celebrating their 50th birthdays along with their wedding, created a complete Oz. The bride was Dorothy, the groom was the Tin Man, and their kids gamely dressed as the Scarecrow, the Cowardly Lion, and the Wicked Witch. The props alone cost $25,000. Guests were asked to come dressed as Munchkins.

When the groom's daughter, complete with a witch's black hat, fake nose, and wrinkles, came down the aisle cackling, "I'll get you, my pretty," guests had to wonder whether she was only following the script.

Another couple was married on Halloween. The bridesmaids wore black witch hats at that one, too. The ushers and the groom himself wore black nail polish and fangs.

If the fangs fit, that's fine. But when wed-

dings require something that unusual, attendants should get a chance to decline. Your daughter has every right to be Snow White. But her friends may not be eager to serve as the seven dwarfs.

This is the time that the mother of the bride can come to the aid of the wedding party. While the bride is within her rights to request hoop skirts or picture hats, you can weigh in on the side of simplicity. There are several ways that brides can show mercy when they pick dresses for their bridesmaids.

◌ Avoid obvious disasters. Large women can look like sausages when they are stuffed into skintight strapless dresses. Small women can look like they are playing dress-up in big frills and flounces.

◌ Make it cheap. Nobody cares about durability and construction in a dress that only has to last through one wearing. If you can find a dress in a nonbridal store, so much the better. Say the word "bridesmaid," and you raise the price by $200. National chains like Ann Taylor often have simple, appropriate dresses at a fraction of the cost.

⚬ Make it individual. Some brides pick a color and a fabric and let the bridesmaids have dresses made in their own style. Several companies offer separates so the bridesmaids can pick tops and skirt styles that flatter their shapes.

⚬ Make it black—the one color a bridesmaid is likely to wear again.

⚬ Skip the matching shoes. The only people looking at the bridesmaids' feet are foot fetishists or small children who can't see above knee level. Neither are likely to be fashion critics offended by unmatched shoes.

⚬ Pay for the dresses for the wedding party. Painful though it may be, keeping good friends is worth the price.

It is unfair to expect the bride to include cousins, in-laws, and other relatives in the bridal party unless she is really close to them. Sisters are a different story. She doesn't have to make her sister the maid or matron of honor, but siblings are always included in the wedding party. This may explain all of the ugly dresses.

What can the bride reasonably expect from her bridesmaids? That they will be happy for her goes without saying. She can also expect them to order their dresses in time for them to be altered before the wedding, to contain their lack of enthusiasm for the attire the bride has selected, to show up before the rehearsal dinner, to provide moral support while the bride's getting dressed, to tell her she looks gorgeous, to be sober enough to walk a straight line down the aisle, to smile for the photographer, and to generally act like they are having a good time at the wedding.

If your daughter wants the bridesmaids to wear a specific necklace or earrings, they should be the bridesmaids' gifts. She can suggest that the bridesmaids get their hair done a certain way, but she may not get the intended results. One bride insisted that all of her bridesmaids have their hair curled. It worked well on the women with long hair, but the one short-haired bridesmaid emerged looking like an uptight grandmother with a bad perm.

Remind your daughter that the bridesmaids are not candidates for extreme makeovers. Asking bridesmaids to dye their hair, lose weight, shape up, or grow a few inches is not likely to endear her to her friends or achieve the desired results. What she sees is what she gets—tattoos, nose rings, orange hair, and all.

The same goes for the groomsmen. The bride cannot suggest that the best man have his unibrow waxed or that the ushers hire personal trainers. She can try to make over the groom, but his friends are off-limits.

Is it fair to expect all of the bridesmaids to attend every shower and bachelorette party? Most brides do expect it. This can be a financial hardship, especially for attendants who live far away. Being in a wedding shouldn't be so expensive that the attendant's most powerful feeling is one of privation, not celebration.

Many bridesmaids are now planning destination bachelorette parties, heading off to Las Vegas or cruising around the Caribbean where they can indulge themselves and the bride. Manicures and pedicures have replaced pub crawls and drinking games as the bachelorette activities of choice—particularly for the bride whose college indulgences are a distant memory. "I am too old to go to a string of bars and wear a veil and run around," said one 35-year-old bride-to-be.

This trend is terrific for the bride who'd rather wake up with a French manicure than a hangover. It enables far-flung wedding parties to meet in a central location to fete the bride. But it puts a further dent in the bridesmaids' budgets since they not only pay for the cost of their trips but also often split the cost of the bride's.

I suggest the adoption of a one-flight rule. If a bridesmaid lives far enough away that she cannot drive to the events, appearance for the wedding weekend should be enough.

In addition, attendants should not be expected to buy more than one gift for the happy couple. As more weddings resemble coronations, guests feel pressured to give gifts that rise to the occasion. Shower gifts are now as expensive as wedding gifts used to be, and wedding gifts are elaborate enough to be trousseaus. No bridesmaid should need to take out a second mortgage to be in a wedding.

In return, the bridesmaids can expect to be invited with a guest, even if they aren't married or engaged. That guest is invited to all of the pre- and postwedding events—it would hardly be fair to expect the boyfriends to cool their heels in the hotel while you entertain the wedding party. The one exception—the escorts can be excluded from a bridesmaids' tea, luncheon, or spa outing unless one of them feels he is in need of emergency exfoliation.

As mother of the bride, you should suggest housing arrangements for your daughter's attendants, but you aren't required to be the housemother for the wedding party. Who sleeps with whom and where is not your concern. Let their mothers worry!

USHERS

Traditionally, the ushers escorted guests to their seats at the ceremony. These days, the guests often fend for themselves. Unless they are instructed to do so, ushers do not usher. They only walk down the aisle as part of the wedding procession. Their chief functions are to rent the selected "monkey suit," to plan and attend the bachelor party, to appear appropriately attired on the day of the wedding, to keep the groom from bolting before the wedding, to walk down the aisle without smirking, to escort the bridesmaids back up the aisle, and to try not to look silly in the wedding pictures.

HONOR ATTENDANTS

Tradition frequently flies out the window when it comes to honor attendants. The bride and groom may select people of either sex to stand up with them. These days, it is unexceptional to have a best woman or a man of honor as long as he doesn't wear a dress and she doesn't wear a tuxedo. There is nothing inherently wrong with cross-dressing, but it does tend to steal attention from the bride.

Traditionally, the maid of honor helps the bride pick her dress, helps address invitations, and hosts a bridal shower. However, when the maid of honor lives out of town or is otherwise unavailable, you have to go to Plan B. As the mother of the bride, you are Plan B.

This is not a hardship because you are probably planning to go wedding-dress shopping with the bride anyway. Many wedding invitations are addressed by a computer, a calligrapher, or calligraphy machine, and the maid of honor probably writes illegibly. However, you don't want to host the bridal shower. This "party" is just a gift grab with food. It is unseemly for the mother of the bride to solicit more loot for her daughter, but you can always recruit a close friend of yours to do it.

The best man makes the first toast to the newlyweds at the wedding reception. In this era of equal opportunity, the maid of honor often makes the second toast. This is a good thing because the best man cannot be counted on to toast the newlyweds. He is more likely to wax eloquent about his friendship with the groom or recite a litany of the groom's most embarrassing moments.

In the first instance, the wedding guests are treated to memories of a friendship that goes back to playground fights in elementary school and has lasted through drunken revels and punishing pickup basketball games. As the best man solemnly intones, "I've got your back" or "I love you, man," it seems crass to mention that he has forgotten the bride altogether.

In the second instance, the best man recalls long-forgotten moments from the groom's early years. At my daughter's wedding, the best man was brother Eddie who revealed that the groom had refused to go to Disney World as a child because he was afraid of Mickey Mouse. At other weddings, I have heard about the groom's checkered romantic past, the girlfriends his friends hated, the girlfriends his parents hated, and the girlfriends who ended up hating him. These are the toasts that make the bride rejoice that she has been forgotten altogether.

As the mother of the bride, you have no control over the toasts. At best, you can encourage the best man to be brief and to remember that there are ladies present. The maid of honor will probably need no coaching. Meredith's maid of honor, Claire, made a toast that was both tasteful and touching. She mentioned me several times.

FLOWER GIRLS, RING BEARERS, AND PETS AS ATTENDANTS

W. C. Fields is said to have said, "Anyone who hates children and dogs can't be all bad." While I would not dream of seconding these curmudgeonly sentiments, it is wise to point out to the bride that there are disadvantages to having children and dogs as members of the wedding party.

The temptation to send an adorable cherub down the aisle is understandable. The outfits are just precious—long, lacy dresses and dainty baskets for flower girls; tiny tuxedos and satin ring pillows for ring bearers, both human and canine. Just be aware that the wearers may not recognize the importance and solemnity of the occasion—or become so overwhelmed by performance anxiety that they throw up and commit other unsocial acts.

At one wedding, the flower girl refused to give up her flower petals. Another little girl got hysterical when she wasn't included in all of the wedding pictures. Her father removed her from the room, but her screams could still be heard as the vows were exchanged.

Ring bearers cannot always be coaxed to come down the aisle or to be quiet once they get to the altar. One young man, imbued with the spirit of the occasion, announced, "I want a dress. I want to marry Grandpa."

Then there was the ring bearer who tossed the ring out of the car window on his way to the church and the ring-bearing dog who lifted a leg at an inappropriate time.

Rehearsing the young attendant cannot duplicate the actual wedding conditions. When the church is filled with people and the music is playing, the young attendant may panic. If the bride really wants to include a small child or two or three, be sure that you build in as many safeguards as you can. Don't dress the flower girl or ring bearer too soon if you want the outfit to stay pristine. Make sure the small fry don't eat too much right before the ceremony—nervous stomachs do disasters make. Be prepared to offer bribes for good behavior.

Most of all, you and the bride need to remember that memories are made of the funny, touching, unexpected, unscripted moments. If that's going to spoil her perfect wedding, leave the kids and the dogs at home.

Reality Check #6

WHO SHOULDN'T BE IN THE WEDDING PARTY

The bride may not want to have very young children in the wedding party for these reasons:

1. They do not take direction well.

2. They are likely to get spooked by the crowd.

3. When they are bad, they are very, very bad. And when they are good, they upstage you.

Your daughter thinks that you are so young, so hip, such a good friend that she'd like you to be a bridesmaid. Before you say "yes," think of these reasons why the mother of the bride should not be a bridesmaid:

1. You won't get to wear a dress that looks really good on you.

2. You'll be up there side by side with all of your daughter's nubile friends.

3. You'll have to go to the bachelorette party. No mother should have to be present when penis-shaped food and party favors are served.

4. Guests will be confused. They may even think that the slut your ex-husband married is the mother of the bride.

Part 2

THE WEDDING PLANS

7

FOR LOVE OR MONEY

And they lived happily ever after . . ." That's the ending you envision for your daughter and the love of her life. The last thing you want is for the newlyweds to return from their honeymoon to a stack of unpaid wedding bills. Many couples spend the first year or two of their marriages paying down their wedding debts.

But what about you? You want to live happily ever after, too. It is easy to get so consumed with wedding planning that you lose sight of the mounting expenses. However, before you've brushed the birdseed—or whatever politically and ecologically correct wedding toss showered the bride and groom—out of your hair, a mountain of bills may be landing on your doorstep.

The average wedding in the United States costs $22,000. Since that average includes the couples who couple-up at city hall and head off for lunch with a few friends, there is a good chance that the cost of your daughter's wedding will be way above the average.

Why do weddings cost so much? A friend of mine attributes it to the "Ralph Laurenization of weddings." Middle-class brides now expect nuptials with a lavishness once confined to the aristocracy.

Benjamin was stunned by the modest budget that I prepared. "That's more than we spent on our first two houses," he said.

"When your daughter gets married, you've got to figure the wedding will cost the same thing as a year in college," a friend told Benjamin. "When your son gets married, it's only a semester."

Or, as another father of the bride put it, "It's like buying an expensive sports car, driving it for five hours, then throwing it over a cliff."

The wedding day has grown into a wedding weekend with multiple events to be arranged and hosted. Rehearsal dinners have been "upgraded" to include all of the out-of-town guests as well as the wedding party. One Florida bride had four parties leading up to her wedding in Jacksonville—including a Mediterranean rehearsal dinner for 117, a Friday-night dinner for 70, and a Middle Eastern buffet luncheon for 375.

The morning after the wedding, she had a Sunday brunch.

"Stay and play" weddings, whether far afield or close to home, reflect another trend. Now that more couples live together before the wedding, the novelty of the wedding night is less compelling. Rather than "alone at last," it's "alone again." So it is not surprising that couples see their wedding weekends as a chance to spend time with families and friends rather than going off by themselves.

One Minnesota couple got married on Maui and took both sets of parents along on their island-hopping honeymoon. The bride filled every day with sightseeing excursions. By the third day, the father of the bride was begging for mercy and hoping the newlyweds would want some alone time so that he could take a nap.

The bride and groom may welcome multiple wedding shindigs and activities as more opportunities to interact with every one of their guests. However, each additional event can approach the cost of the wedding itself. In some cases, other friends or relatives host the "warm-up" parties. The uncle of a New York groom ferried 185 guests to a party on Ellis Island. They were served a 10-course dinner while a band played.

With a warm-up like that, who needs a wedding! Imagine the pressure that mother of the bride must have felt!

Even without such posh preliminaries, there is pressure to ratchet up in every area—more courses, more flowers, hand calligraphy on the invitations.

Caterers even claim that people eat more at weddings. This makes no sense. Everyone is wearing fancy, formfitting clothes that discourage overeating. The guests don't get to order what they like. The wedding feast is constantly interrupted by dancing and other rituals. And, if you dare to leave the table, a waiter whisks your half-eaten plate of food away.

What caterers really mean is that brides are conned into ordering more food at weddings—much of which is wasted.

Weddings also inspire a lot of nonwedding expenditures. It isn't fair to include them in the wedding budget, but you're bound to incur some additional expenses like the cost of your personal trainer for six months, the price of a new tuxedo for the father of the bride, or your dancing lessons.

That's fine, if you can afford it. But now that brides are marrying later in life, parents of brides are more likely to be nearing retirement age when their daughters say "I do." Do you really want to keep working well into your 70s to pay for your daughter's dream wedding?

There are alternatives. If they are willing and able, you can split the cost of the wedding with the groom's parents and the couple themselves. You can offer the couple a hefty sum to elope. It's bound to be cheaper than an actual wedding. Or you can work with the bride and groom to create a budget for a wedding you can afford.

There is an assumption that, when it comes to weddings, common sense flies out the window on wings of love. Many mothers of brides seem to believe that weddings always operate like the Pentagon—cost overruns are inevitable.

It ain't necessarily so! You can make a wedding budget and stick to it, as long as you estimate costs realistically and operate on a zero-tolerance rule. That means "just say no." Draw a line in the sand. Pick the tough cliché of your choice and stick to it. Once you exceed your agreed-upon budget in any way, it is easier to justify the next splurge and the next splurge and the expense after that.

Start with your mother-daughter pre-nup. That agreement spells out who is going to pay the bills and what the grand total will be. Then you and your daughter should use the budget sheets in a bridal magazine or on a wedding Web site to create a preliminary wedding budget. These worksheets help you cover all of the bases. But don't trust their estimates on the cost of photography, flowers, and other services. Unless you live in Timbuktu, you'll have to pay more for everything associated with the wedding.

For example, theknot.com estimated that Meredith would need $1,658.18 for photography. In the Washington, D.C., area, many photographers charge triple that amount. Some of the well-known shooters won't take off their lens caps for less than $7,000 to $10,000.

The wedding industry breaks down the typical wedding budget this way:

Reception—50 percent

That includes the site, catering, bar and beverages, wedding cake, parking, and transportation.

 Music—10 percent

 Flowers—10 percent

 Wedding attire—10 percent

That includes only clothing for the bride and groom.

 Photography—10 percent

 Stationery—4 percent

That includes invitations, announcements, thank-you notes, postage, programs, and placecards.

 Extras—6 percent (at least)

That includes attendants' gifts, favors, rehearsal dinner, wedding rings, marriage license, officiant fees, and church or synagogue fees.

These allocations may not mesh with the bride's priorities. What does she care most about? Food? Music? A place big enough to accommodate all of the Tri-Delts from University of Wisconsin in Oshkosh?

My daughter put the setting at the top of her list. She wanted to be married in a garden. We paid more than we planned to rent the atrium at the botanical gardens operated by the Northern Virginia Regional Park Authority. The gardens were beautiful and the atrium has trees and flowers growing inside, so weather would not be a problem. We also saved on flowers because there was no need to decorate the room. The park authority had planned the facility for weddings. It was equipped with tables, chairs, and a catering kitchen, which saved us the cost of rentals.

We also splurged on photography and food. That meant economizing on reception music—hiring a deejay instead of a band. We had a simple wedding cake, baked by the caterer. The invitations were printed, not engraved, and the envelopes were addressed by machine. I would have shot the first person who dared to mention chair covers.

"Spend money on memories," one wise wedding planner advises her clients. "A fantastic photographer is your best investment." After that, she stresses the site and the music. Food is less important, she believes. "Most people come to a wedding to party. They are drinking. As long as the food is good and beautifully presented, it doesn't have to cost a lot."

Once you get estimates for the things that matter most, plug those numbers into the budget and see how much money you have to spend on everything else. You'll soon find yourself over budget—on paper, at least. That's when you and the bride have to start paring down the low-priority items and eliminating nonessentials.

Your daughter may say that everything is essential. But if you show that you are serious about sticking to a budget, the two of you will find ways to cut.

For example, favors aren't essential. Ask the bride to think of the favors she's collected at the weddings she's attended. Weren't they all impractical, insipid, or fattening?

Food is essential. Regardless of the hour of the day or night, wedding guests expect to be fed. If you are serving anything stronger than lemonade, you want to feed them. Otherwise they begin to teeter, bellow, and commit unsocial acts. These can result in damage to their reputations and, more important from your perspective, damage to property for which you can and will be held responsible.

However, you are not required to serve food in such quantities that guests have trouble getting up from the table or to offer a midnight snack when the final dinner course was served after 10:00 p.m. This is a wedding, not a cruise!

Chairs are a necessity. Chair covers with bows that match the bridal color scheme are not.

Invitations are a necessity. Engraved invitations in double envelopes and protective tissue are not.

The groom's family is a necessity, even if they are not contributing one dime toward the cost of the wedding. The groom's father's business associates are not.

This book has lots of suggestions for identifying nonessentials and keeping expenses reasonable. It is all a matter of your mind-set.

Think like a rich person. Celebrities and other people with lots of money never buy when they can borrow. They borrow houses and estates for their weddings. They borrow dresses and jewelry all the time. Actor Adam Sandler got married at Dick Clark's Malibu estate. Former New York mayor Rudy Guiliani got married at the mayoral mansion even though he didn't live there anymore. It is perfectly acceptable to borrow anything but the groom.

Think like a guest. Have you ever been at a party and heard someone say, "I had a terrible time; I hated the flowers" or "No palate-cleansing sorbet? I'm outta here"? Guests come to celebrate with you. They couldn't care less about the table linens or the aisle runner. Guests have no idea what you could have done. Ending the reception an hour earlier than you might have will save you money, and no one will know the difference. We asked that champagne for toasting the bride and groom be offered, but not automatically poured. Why serve champagne to people who won't drink it?

Play the numbers. If you can cut back

on the number of bridesmaids and groomsmen, you have fewer to feed at the rehearsal dinner, fewer guests at the reception, and fewer attendants' gifts to buy.

Save the day. You can get much more for your money if you don't have the wedding on Saturday night. Pick an unpopular wedding month—January, February, or March—and you'll find vendors much more amenable to negotiation.

Think nonwedding. Say the word "wedding" and the price goes up. Do those disposable cameras on the tables for guests have to be wedding white? You'll pay extra for that. Do you really need the hairstylist to come to your site? You'll pay more for the same style you'd get at the salon.

Save on the ceremony. All eyes will be on the bride, so you can cut back on the scenery. For example, we were married under a canopy of leaves instead of flowers.

We saved the flower budget for the bridal bouquet—which showed in the wedding pictures—and the table arrangements. If the wedding is taking place in a beautiful church or synagogue, there's no need to embellish it with flowers. Nobody notices the wedding ceremony music unless it is really terrible, so go for as few musicians as possible.

Sweat the small stuff. Little expenses mushroom at weddings. Little savings also add up. Unless they are lace heirlooms, wedding veils all tend to look alike. It doesn't pay to buy an expensive one—particularly because most brides shed their veils right after the ceremony. Wedding purses and shoes are rarely worth what they cost. I've never seen a bride actually carry a purse. Why would she need one, unless she was packing mad money and keys to a getaway car?

Reality Check # 7

7 QUESTIONABLE WAYS TO SAVE ON THE WEDDING

1. Selling ads in the wedding program

2. Charging for drinks at the reception

3. Hiring your son to park cars, then charging for valet parking

4. Buying plastic flowers for the bridal bouquet

5. Inviting all of your customers or clients so you can deduct the wedding as a business expense

6. Trying to marry off two of your daughters at the same time to save on invitations, and so on

7. "Splitting" costs with the groom's family so that you actually make a profit on the wedding

THE WEDDING PLANNER

The bride grew up in Washington, D.C., a city renowned for its Japanese cherry trees. Unfortunately, she wasn't getting married during cherry blossom season. So the New York florist had to fly in branches of cherry blossoms from Canada to create the ambience this Washington bride wanted. A set designer collaborated on the bride's "magical garden" theme. The reception featured an oxygen bar and cigar maker rolling smokes for the guests.

This is the kind of wedding that no mere mortal could create. This is an affair that cries out for an impresario. In other words, a wedding planner.

No self-respecting celebrity gets married without one. They may be barefoot on the beach, but you can bet that a wedding planner raked the sand and arranged to have the clouds floating overhead two by two.

Even if you don't want to have your chapel transformed into a renaissance courtyard the way Wynonna Judd did or have a yarmulke designed for your bulldog á la Adam Sandler, you may want to hire a wedding planner to handle some or all of the wedding details.

A wedding planner is many things to many mothers of brides. The planner can come up with the ideas for the wedding or implement the ideas of the bride. The planner may have a stable of vendors she routinely works with or can suggest vendors to be considered. The planner can be with you from buying the dress to sealing the honeymoon suitcases or show up only on the wedding day to coordinate the ceremony and the reception. The planner can create a budget or work within the budget you create. Some charge a flat fee; some charge a percentage of the wedding.

If your daughter wants her version of a cherry blossom and oxygen bar extravaganza, and you are prepared to pay for it, you need a wedding producer. This kind of planner meets with you to create a concept and then runs with it. She knows people at the hotels and resorts as well as caterers, florists, musicians, calligraphers, lighting designers, and people who do things you don't even know you need doing. For example, a wedding producer can find a lighting genius who'll create all kinds of special effects from landscape lighting to moving images and shapes projected against the walls.

Remember Martin Short in *Father of the Bride* or Jennifer Lopez in *The Wedding Planner*? They were producers. For a producer to mastermind your high-concept wedding, you can pay upward of $40,000 for the planner alone.

But if you're planning to cover the walls of the Beverly Hills Hotel ballroom in fabric so it looks more like a living room, the way wedding-planner-to-the-stars Mindy Weiss did for the wedding of Shaquille O'Neal and Shaunie Nelson, the planning fee feels like a pittance. Shaq also had his wedding ceremony in a tent in the hotel's garden. The tent alone had five vintage chandeliers, carpet on the floor, and dotted swiss covers on the chairs. No wonder Shaq rewrote the traditional vows to say, "For richer and for richer."

If you are thinking about a little less opulence, or a lot less opulence, you may still want a full-service wedding planner. This is an events pro who can help you put together a budget, steer you to the right vendors, help you negotiate contracts, and be there the day of the wedding to direct the proceedings.

A wedding planner should help you decide how to spend your money wisely. The planner can tell you that roses are actually one of the most economical wedding flowers and that you may be better off contracting for an all-inclusive beverage budget rather than paying for actual consumption. (Some vendors pad their beverage fees by opening bottles of wine willy-nilly, according to one savvy wedding planner.)

Hiring a full-service wedding planner gives you access to specialists you would have a hard time finding on your own. They know craftsmen who can build props—a trellis for a garden look or a tabletop Eiffel Tower for the couple who will always have Paris. They can find an authentic African headdress or a seamstress who will create one. They work with lighting designers, specialty cake bakers, and entertainers.

Like a wedding producer, a wedding planner has ongoing relationships with hotel catering managers, florists, and photographers. These are relationships you cannot duplicate on your own. Every vendor you hire should want to walk through fire for your daughter, the bride. In truth, you may be only a one-time client to these people. The person they'll really want to please is your wedding planner. To them, she means repeat business. They may offer her a better deal or throw in a few extras just to keep her happy.

A full-service planner will create a time line for the wedding day itself and make sure the vendors stick to it. She'll keep the wedding party in line and handle sticky issues for you. If one of the bridesmaids is accessorized like a Christmas tree, the wedding planner will strip off the excess jewelry. If somebody's baby starts howling, she'll gently lead the parents toward the nearest exit.

You can expect to pay a full-service planner 10 to 15 percent of the wedding budget. On the other hand, you won't have to pay a therapist to help you handle your anxiety over all of the details.

A mother of the bride may be very comfortable planning the wedding but may not want to spend the wedding day running the show. A day-of-wedding planner can take over so that you can be a guest and enjoy the party. She'll be the one to bark orders to the flower girl who refuses to unhand her petals.

You can expect the day-of-wedding planner to want to start working up to a month in advance. She'll need time to get to know your vendors, make sure you've arranged for everything that needs arranging, and establish a schedule for the wedding events.

What's important isn't what she does—it's what you don't have to do. "I never knew that the groom had left the wedding programs in his car," one mother of the bride said. "The planner arranged to go get them. She did everything." Day-of-wedding planners usually charge a flat fee, anywhere from $1,500 to $6,000.

Many hotels and wedding venues have their own wedding planners. That is both the good news and the bad news. They come at no additional cost, they know vendors who know their facility, and they may have great ideas. On the other hand, your contract is with the facility, not the planner. One mother of the bride dealt with three different hotel planners in the course of arranging her wedding.

Before you hire a wedding planner, you need to think about more than her fee. Wedding planners are bossy by nature. Do you and your daughter really like this person and trust her to fulfill your daughter's dream? A planner can gently steer you in the right direction, but you don't want to be steamrollered.

"We were new to the area and I felt clueless," one mother of the bride explained. "The wedding planner introduced us to vendors I would never have found. She also clued us into the budget realities. It was worth it to get the hand-holding."

But the bride and groom couldn't stand the wedding planner. They felt she was overbearing, a prima donna. She wasn't creative, and she wasn't listening to them.

When the planner and the couple couldn't agree on save-the-date cards, the bride and groom bought their own. The bride hated the favors that the planner found. Eventually the mother of the bride found other favors, but they had to pay for the planner's favors even though they never used them.

If you know of anyone who needs 200 little mesh bags that can be filled with candy, I can get them for you at a good price.

When you and your daughter don't agree, a wedding planner can help you find a middle ground—or another solution altogether. But don't expect the wedding planner to automatically side with you even if she is closer to your age than your daughter's. She has watched weddings evolve over the years, so she is more comfortable with strapless wedding dresses and male bridal attendants than you are likely to be. She's seen it all.

But if she starts telling war stories, find another planner. You don't want her telling the next bride-to-be or mother of the bride about you.

Reality Check #8

10 SIGNS YOU NEED A WEDDING PLANNER

1. The last time you invited six people for dinner, it took you a week to recover.

2. Your idea of organization is "I know it's here somewhere."

3. You are so overbooked that you have to pencil in time to sleep.

4. You and your daughter can't agree on whether the sky is cerulean or aquamarine.

5. You live in Seattle and your daughter lives in Secaucus.

6. You live in Secaucus and your daughter is getting married in the Seychelles.

7. To achieve the "ambience" that the bride requested, you're going to need a lighting designer, a set designer, and Steven Spielberg.

8. The bride and groom would like to include authentic Tahitian customs in the wedding because they both love Gauguin.

9. The groom's family are vegans, and the bride wants a barbecue.

10. In the virtual certainty that something will go wrong, you want to have somebody else to blame.

9

LOCATION, LOCATION, LOCATION

The wedding venue ranks right up there with the groom and the dress in order of importance. The site sets the whole tone of the wedding and dictates many of the details. It is a big—if not the biggest—chunk of the budget. It is also the object of many of your daughter's wedding fantasies.

As a little girl, my daughter dreamed of getting married in a castle. Thank goodness she outgrew that idea. But she still wanted to play out the "most important day of her life" in a place of charm and grace, a setting worthy of her great romance.

Living in Washington, we are near some very grand event spaces. Unfortunately, the White House was not available. We could have rented several marble museums, the atrium of the Ronald Reagan International Trade Center, or a baroque mansion frequented by diplomats. Of course, the cost of renting one of these impressive locations would have meant serving the guests Kool-Aid and Cheez Doodles.

Meredith also ruled out hotel ballrooms—too formal and too sterile, she said. Knowing what it would cost to use the top-drawer hotels in town, I happily agreed.

Our area has more than its share of ancestral homes and other historic settings. However, we soon discovered that the more historic they are, the more likely they were to have rooms too small to accommodate more than 80 to 100 people. Invite more people than that and you have to split them up in different rooms or erect a tent on the grounds.

The more we talked about locations, the clearer Meredith's vision was to me. My daughter dreamed of getting married in a flower-filled garden on a balmy evening in June. No matter that evenings in June where we live tend to include excessive heat or unseasonable cold, bugs, and thunderstorms.

The majority of brides want to be married outdoors. Since weddings cannot be postponed or rescheduled if it rains, you want to be sure that there is an indoor alternative at the outdoor site you select.

For us, the issue was moot. We were lucky enough to find a venue that brought a garden inside—a flower-filled atrium in a botanical garden. Other mothers might be able to take the vagaries of weather in stride. But I had suffered through too many outdoor disasters to trust Mother Nature.

I had been to outdoor weddings where we watched each other's makeup melt in Washington's humidity. I had shivered or huddled under tent flaps while the thunder roared and the rain poured. At one ceremony, the storm was so loud, the bride and groom had to shout their vows. At other weddings, the guests went inside and out several times, dodging wind and rain, because the brides wanted to get married in the garden, on the waterfront, or in sight of the city skyline. Even when the indoor alternatives had windows overlooking the scenic vista, these brides wanted to be outdoors.

My fears were well-founded. Sure enough, the month Meredith married could have been called the "month of the monsoon." It rained so much that we feared roads might be closed. The wedding day dawned cloudy, but hours later, it cleared. We dared to set up outside for the ceremony. As soon as the chairs were in place, we felt the first raindrops. We hastily moved indoors and stayed there. Guests did go outside for cocktails, and we did get to take lots of pictures in the gardens with our makeup intact and our hair unfrizzed.

There are lots of places—both public and private—to hold weddings. Creative couples keep coming up with more of them. Weddings have been held at the Country Music Hall of Fame in Nashville and even at the Green-Wood Historic Chapel in Green-Wood Cemetery in Brooklyn. One couple arranged to wed near the graves of maestro Leonard Bernstein, Boss Tweed, and artist Jean-Michel Basquiat.

Your daughter can plight her troth at a colonial Spanish garrison in San Juan, Puerto Rico, sashay down the aisle of the Cowgirl Museum and Hall of Fame in Fort Worth, or toast her groom at a Napa Valley winery. One book on unusual weddings, *201 Unique Ways to Make Your Wedding Special,* suggests the bride consider an aquarium, a presidential library, a saloon, an ice rink, a pawn shop, or the Hoover Dam. Author Don Altman also mentions a jail as a possible wedding venue—he does not specify whether either bride or groom needs to be a resident at the time.

Here are some of the more mainstream options.

Hotels and catering facilities are the easiest and often the most cost-effective wedding venues. They have ballrooms or banquet halls large enough to accommodate your guests. You don't have to bring in a staff of cooks, servers, and bartenders or rent tables, chairs, china, linens, and the rest of the event paraphernalia. Hotels usually have an events coordinator to help plan and pull off your grand affair. They are accessible for people with disabilities, and bathrooms are always nearby. Hotels can also house the out-of-town guests, so you don't have to worry about transporting them to the wedding.

Hotels don't have the same restrictions that other venues often impose. You can party into the wee hours, serve flaming desserts, and shape the celebration any way you want. Many have patios or gardens for outdoor ceremonies.

If you require a very special menu, some hotels will let you bring in outside food. For example, an Indian couple selected a hotel in Montreal that allowed them to have the wedding dinner catered by a favorite Indian restaurant. Since many of the 250 to 300 wedding guests were coming from overseas and staying at the wedding hotel, it was a winning arrangement for both the bridal couple and the hotel management. Hotels that don't have kosher kitchens will usually arrange with a kosher caterer to bring in meals for guests who require them.

Plan to visit several hotels and interview the banquet staff before you select one. You can't tell from the brochure where the ballroom is located. Some ballrooms are dark and below ground; some are sunny with big windows. You also want to know what other parties are taking place on the day of the wedding. Are back-to-back ballrooms going to host your daughter's wedding and a convention of college fraternity presidents? It's a good idea to go to lunch or dinner there to test the quality of the food and service, the cleanliness of the public areas, and the overall ambience of the place. Check out the guest rooms, too, since your friends and relatives may want to stay there.

Before you sign a contract with a hotel, be sure you understand all of the charges you'll incur. For example, if they don't bake the wedding cake, they may charge you for cutting it. You don't want to get on the bad side of a banquet manager carrying a large carving knife!

Resorts and country inns are also popular wedding venues. They share the advantages of hotels but may have more charm. Resorts also offer lots of activities for guests so you don't have to worry about entertaining the out-of-towners. The only problem may be getting out-of-town guests to the resort location.

Museums are increasingly becoming popular wedding venues. For example, actor Edward Burns and model Christy Turlington chose the Asian Art Museum, in San Francisco, for their big day. Many museums have grand staircases and dramatic galleries that make wonderful wedding backdrops. With all of the art or objects on display, you don't need much decoration. In addition, guests can walk through the exhibits.

Major art museums aren't the only spaces you can consider. The Baltimore Museum of Industry, the Wadsworth Atheneum, in Hartford, Connecticut, and the Fernbank Museum of Natural History, in Atlanta, all hosted weddings recently. At the Fernbank, dinner was served in the Great Hall, a four-story, sky-lit atrium decorated with enormous dinosaur replicas. At Seattle's newest museum, the Experience Music Project, you can celebrate in your own sound lab.

Museums do have limits on when you can have the space, what you can cook, what you can serve, how you can arrange tables, and so on. You may have to take out an insurance bond, choose from a list of approved vendors, and stay away from red wine or cranberry juice, beverages likely to leave stains. Private affairs can't be held during the museum's operating hours, and your vendors can't start setting up until the museum closes. Museums are built to please the eye, not the ear, so the acoustics can be strange. Also, bathrooms may be far from the reception site.

Museums can have arcane rules. At the Corcoran Gallery of Art, in Washington, D.C., anyone drinking a beverage out of a bottle is busted. Candles are out of the question—although you may get away with tiny votives.

It will come as no surprise that, unless you are a major donor, you'll have to pay handsomely for the privilege of using a museum. The American Museum of Natural History in New York City charges $25,000 for a seated reception. But that's New York! Dining with dinosaurs is cheaper outside the Big Apple.

Parks and historic properties. Every community has historic homes, estates, chapels, schoolhouses, mills, and taverns. Many have been restored by local trusts or parks authorities and are maintained by revenues from party rentals. They can make wonderful backdrops for weddings.

For example, Cabell's Mill, in Centreville, Virginia, was a working gristmill that was later turned into a guest house. Franklin Delano Roosevelt slept there. The San Diego Department of Parks and Recreation operates a Victorian village, a historic garden, an adobe, and several pavilions that are used for weddings. Southern belles can choose any number of plantation houses and antebellum mansions like Little Gardens in Lawrenceville, Georgia, or the 1898 courthouse in Decatur.

These facilities often have tables and chairs and warming kitchens, if not full catering kitchens. However, they often have restrictions. For example, the atrium where Meredith got married closes at 1:00 a.m.

We had to be out by midnight so the caterers would have time to clean up. The rental fee covered a five-hour time period. We bought an extra hour before the event so we could come in early for pictures.

To find public gardens in your area, you can check the American Association of Botanical Gardens and Arboreta Web site, www.aabga.org.

Clubs can be one of the best deals around for weddings. If someone in the family is an active or retired military officer, you can hold the wedding at any officers' club in your area. Golf clubs, tennis clubs, and yacht clubs are obvious choices. But you may not think of university clubs, fraternal buildings, and other facilities. Sometimes they happily rent to nonmembers. Just be sure to have a meal there before you commit to anything—food is not necessarily a club's highest priority. They may have spent a fortune on a gorgeous golf course and scrimped on the club's kitchen.

Colleges and universities usually have both chapels and reception facilities. You may need to be an alum to use the chapel, but rules are usually looser for college conference centers and other buildings. If you have to use campus catering, be sure to eat there in advance. Lots of colleges contract out with big catering companies. You don't want mystery meat, succotash, or any of the other specialties that make even college students gag at your wedding. You also want to check the campus alcohol policy before you order champagne for your reception. Imagine campus rent-a-cops busting the guests at the reception.

Vineyards are hosting more and more weddings. Wineries can be colorful with a lot of rustic charm, the countryside is beautiful, and the beverage of choice is close at hand. They may not have a party planner on staff, so you'll have to hire one or become one for the duration. If indoor facilities are limited, you may need a tent or two. You'll also need to find vendors in the area—particularly a caterer and a florist. One thing you won't have to worry about—running low on wine.

Weddings on the water are also increasing in popularity. Yachts, riverboats, schooners, and tour boats are eager to sail newlyweds and their guests off into the sunset. You can even rent the former presidential yacht, the USS *Sequoia,* for a wedding cruise on the Potomac and see the mail slot President Kennedy had built into the bedroom so staffers bringing official papers wouldn't interrupt any trysts.

Shipboard weddings can offer breathtaking backdrops. Imagine exchanging vows with the Statue of Liberty looking on! Some also boast luxury accoutrements. *Inamorata,* operated by World Yacht in New York, has an executive chef, a bridal suite, a decorative fireplace, and a spiral staircase for the bride's dramatic entrance.

Smooth sailing for the bride and groom cannot be guaranteed, however. Rough seas can mean flying food, sliding wedding cake, and the bride and groom holding onto each other for dear life during the ceremony. The bride will be advised to wear low heels and skip the train. Sometimes the crew may hand out antiseasickness bracelets. Latecomers either delay the ceremony or get left behind at the dock. And guests can't sneak away early.

Home sweet home is one wedding venue without a rental fee. You can pick any date and be assured that the place will be available. And the location certainly has unique sentimental charm. But you need a big enough house or a lawn large enough for a tent. If you do want to use the house, you'll probably have to move the furniture out.

Don't expect to save money by hosting the wedding at home, according to party planners. You'll need to rent tables, chairs, china, silverware, glassware, and linens. You'll need to pay for trash removal, ice, lighting, and audiovisual equipment. You'll want to rent bathrooms, too. (Don't worry about sending your well-dressed guests off to industrial portable toilets. At a wedding I attended last year, the portal bathrooms were marble, mirrored, and so elegant that even guests who didn't have to use them went just to see them.)

Plan also on sprucing up the house and grounds before the wedding, then repairing the damage done by vendors and guests afterward.

Is it worth it? For better or worse, there's no place like home.

Reality Check #9

QUESTIONS TO ASK YOURSELF BEFORE YOU HOST A WEDDING AT HOME

1. Friends describe your house as:

   a. Baronial
   b. Rambling and rustic
   c. Great for growing children
   d. Likely to be condemned

2. Before the wedding will you have to:

   a. Paint the house
   b. Landscape the yard
   c. Resod the lawn
   d. Get rid of your rottweiler
   e. Get rid of your live-in gangster brother
   f. Buy a new house

3. If you don't invite the neighbors, can you still:

   a. Park cars on their lawn
   b. Park your dog in their yard
   c. Play loud music after midnight
   d. Send guests next door to use the bathroom
   e. Store extra ice in their freezer
   f. Wait until they leave on vacation, and launch fireworks from their patio

4. Nobody in your neighborhood will call the police unless:

   a. You play loud music after midnight
   b. A wedding guest tramples their tulips
   c. You fail to pay protection

5. After the wedding, you'll have to:

   a. Paint the house
   b. Relandscape the yard
   c. Resod the lawn
   d. Move

10

WELCOME TO FANTASY ISLAND

Destination weddings are all about fantasy. The bride sees herself and her beloved literally going off into the sunset or schussing down the ski slopes hand in hand. If your daughter wants a destination wedding, she is asking you to share her fantasy.

First you have to accept the fact that she's not going to walk down the aisle at home. Then you'll have to deal with your different views of her wedding vision.

~ She sees the romance of a ceremony on the sand. You wonder how you're going to get Grandma down to the beach.

~ She sees moonlight and roses. You calculate the cost of shipping roses to the Rockies in mid-February.

~ She's thinking Bermuda breezes. You're thinking Bermuda Triangle.

You are both right. But between the two of you, you can make most of her wedding dream come true. You don't want to rain on her parade, although you may have to remind her that Mother Nature might.

It is easier to share the fantasy when you realize the practical advantages of destination weddings. Far-flung families may find it easier to gather at a resort where they can spend days together. Battling and bitter exes can be sent to different hotels. Cultural and religious differences are smoothed over—the wedding reflects the traditions of Tahiti or Tuscany rather than that of either family. If either the bride or groom has been married before, a destination wedding may be more comfortable than a "been there, done that" traditional affair.

It's easier to limit the guest list for a destination wedding. You won't offend friends, colleagues, and distant relatives if you don't invite them. Only your nearest and dearest will be willing to trek to the magnificent middle of nowhere to watch the couple take their vows. You can always give a party for all of your other friends and relatives at home at a later date to fete the newlyweds.

You may be tempted to invite a lot of people, assuming they couldn't possibly come, but they will send wedding presents.

However, if the bride picks a great location at a great time, you can't count on as many no-shows. When the daughter of a Washington television anchor got married in Vail, Colorado, at the height of ski season, 300 people made the trip.

On the other hand, the happy couple has to be realistic about how many friends and relatives will follow them to the ends of the earth. Grandparents can't be expected to sit on the frozen pews in an ice cathedral or jump into an all-terrain vehicle at Camp Jeep. Pregnant friends aren't going to trek through the wilds of Wyoming or West Virginia.

Fairy-tale weddings sometimes have very real limitations. Every girl is entitled to feel like Cinderella on her wedding day. If she gets married at the Disneyland Hotel, in Anaheim, California, she can even arrive at her fairy-tale wedding in Cinderella's crystal coach with a white horse and two costumed footmen and pledge her love in front of

Sleeping Beauty's castle. But she can do the "I dos" in Disneyland only after Labor Day, before Memorial Day, and on a Sunday night when the park closes early. Cinderella's coach has only limited availability and will be cancelled in inclement weather. Add to that the inconvenience of driving in it after it turns into a pumpkin at midnight. Those pumpkin seeds are murder on the dress.

No matter where your daughter gets married, one thing is certain. You can rest assured that even if the groom and the guests are dressed in board shorts and T-shirts, your daughter will get to wear the wedding gown of her dreams. She may be barefoot or in ski boots, but it wouldn't be a fantasy wedding if the bride couldn't dress like a princess.

Like most things in life, a simple, little wedding far from home is much more complicated than it looks. You and your daughter will have to start planning well in advance, give guests much more notice than the usual six to eight weeks, and stay on top of more details than you would if the wedding was in your own backyard.

First, find out what is required to get legally married. Wedding regulations vary from country to country. If you're planning a wedding abroad, you'll need to check legal requirements with the U.S. embassy or tourist bureau.

Some countries have strict residency requirements. Are the bride and groom ready to move to Montmartre for 60 days before the wedding? Do they have 30 days to spend in Tahiti as a prewedding honeymoon? Mexico requires a blood test in the town in which you marry. In Thailand, a Buddhist monk will only bless the wedding ceremony if it takes place before 11:00 a.m. You may need to have all your paperwork and identity documents like birth certificates translated into another language and go through lots of inexplicable bureaucratic red tape to make the marriage happen.

Don't plan a shipboard ceremony—contrary to popular lore, a ship's captain can't perform a legal marriage ceremony. Cruise weddings are fine as long as the official ceremony takes place in port.

Frankly, it is much easier if the couple slips into your local courthouse for a legal marriage here at home and just goes through the motions on location.

In the United States, every city and county has different rules about marriage licenses. The marriage license must be issued by the jurisdiction where the wedding takes place, even if it's just a stone's throw away from where you live. And the officiant must be licensed there, too.

Of course, the easiest place to pull off a wedding is Las Vegas. The clerk's office at the courthouse is open seven days a week until midnight and 24 hours a day on holidays. The couple just pays $55 for a marriage license, picks a chapel, and says "I do." There are more than 100 chapels and no waiting. One chapel offers drive-through weddings for lovers so eager to wed that they don't want to wait the time it takes to climb out of the car. No wonder Clark County issued 120,000 marriage licenses in 2003 alone!

Find a wedding coordinator. Even the most-organized bride or mother of the bride faces incredible challenges planning a wedding far from home. That is why every "destination" resort has a wedding coordinator or a catering manager who doubles as a wedding planner. They usually offer wedding packages that include the officiant, the flowers, the food, the music, and all the bells and whistles.

Hawaii is so popular for destination weddings that on the island of Maui alone,

59,000 couples tied the knot in five months of 2003—and that was in the off-season. So it is not surprising that Maui resorts are geared up to fulfill bridal fantasies.

For example, at the Sheraton Maui on Kaanapali Beach, your daughter can get the Pu'u Keka'a Ali'i wedding package. It includes:

- Assistance in obtaining the marriage license
- A ceremony on the Ali'i lawn, an officiant to perform it, and a Hawaiian musical duo
- A wedding arch with fresh flowers and a floral bridal path
- Cascading bouquet or flower leis
- A two-tiered wedding cake and a souvenir silver cake server
- Personalized champagne flutes
- Three nights' accommodations in the Ali'i suite with breakfast buffet
- A bottle of Dom Perignon champagne
- A photo album
- A romantic dinner for two under the stars

The hotel can also arrange to have butterflies released at the end of the ceremony.

A wedding planner at a Hawaiian resort will do almost anything to fulfill a bridal fantasy. To add drama to the wedding ceremony, the resort can get you a conch shell blower or a hula dancer. They can also stage a royal Hawaiian wedding procession for your princess.

But there are limits. A wedding coordinator can get you a rabbi, a minister, or a judge for your location ceremony. However, a Catholic ceremony must take place in a church.

One bride demanded to arrive at her beach wedding in a canoe and be carried ashore by a fat Hawaiian. She expected the hotel to furnish the canoe and the fat Hawaiian. The coordinator at the Maui Sheraton flatly refused. The water is too rough at that point of the island and . . . well, let's just say that the bride wouldn't be getting a local award for cultural sensitivity.

You don't have to use a resort coordinator. There are 80 to 100 independent wedding planners on Maui alone. Just make sure that you and your daughter do your homework. Given the fact that Hawaii is several thousand miles and several time zones away from most paying customers, some "planners" have been known to disappear with the wedding deposits.

There are also travel companies that specialize in destination weddings. For example, Scottishweddingsonline.com can get you everything but the bride, the groom, and your own clan for a highland wedding. Would your daughter like to get married on a mountaintop in New Zealand? No

problem. A helicopter can deliver the happy couple to the site, and a local shepherd will pronounce them "husband and wife." It is all arranged through nzweddingservices.co.nz. Other sites, like theweddingexperience.com, Italian-weddings.com, and weddings-in-fiji.com offer similar services. What's more, on Fiji, the bride can arrive by water and be carried to the beach by "warriors'" in grass skirts. Whatever floats the bride's boat! Perhaps the Hawaiian bride just picked the wrong Fantasy Island.

Closer to home, Las Vegas is attractive to many couples because it is easy to get to from all over the country. Also, the bride and groom don't have to worry about inventing activities to amuse their guests before and after the wedding.

Mention Las Vegas wedding and visions of Elvis impersonators dance in your head. Certainly the city is ready to fulfill every kitschy fantasy from a ceremony at the top of the Eiffel Tower at the Paris Las Vegas hotel to a "gondola cruise" at the Venetian. If you hold the wedding in the Studio 54 nightclub in the MGM Grand, the bride can descend from the ceiling on a swing.

But Las Vegas also caters to more traditional tastes. At the posh Bellagio Resort, there are two wedding chapels with hand-painted wooden panels, Venetian glass windows, and handblown gas chandeliers. When the daughter of a Hollywood mogul was married there awhile back, a scenic designer re-created a scene from a Monet painting. The bridal party was gowned in the colors of water lilies.

Your own local wedding planners may be able to make the arrangements for a destination wedding. If you would rather do it yourself, local tourist boards may be able to help you find wedding sites and resources. Just be sure that you get references for the vendors you select, that all contracts with vendors are detailed, and that you know about taxes and "extras." After all, you are buying services without tasting the canapés or the cake, listening to the live music, or meeting the minister.

Get more than a picture. Booking a wedding venue sight unseen can be a risky business. It can be like buying a house based on the picture. You can see the lovely garden surrounding the house, but you can't see the landfill across the street. You need to ask *a lot* of questions and, if possible, talk to someone who has visited the site.

A sunset wedding is lovely—if your wedding site faces in the right direction to see it. The view of the red rocks around Sedona, the Grand Canyon, or Niagara Falls may be breathtaking, but if your ceremony is in a ballroom without windows, you could just as easily be in downtown Dubuque. Before you book that wedding on the beach, find out if it is open to the public. I attended one wedding in Maui because I happened to be wandering by when the ceremony took place. Luckily, I was wearing my formal flip-flops at the time.

Brides can get so caught up in their own wedding fantasy that they lose touch with reality. One young woman arrived in Hawaii a day before her wedding, took one look at the wedding site, and asked, "Are there going to be bugs here tomorrow?" Another arrived on a gorgeous afternoon and demanded the same weather for her wedding day.

Fantasy Island can be a nightmare during hurricane season. When the wind started howling and the rain came down in sheets, one bridal party turned on the resort wedding coordinator. Surely, she could have prevented the storm if she tried!

Ready, set, send. The more stuff you can ship to the wedding site in advance, the less you'll have to worry about just before the wedding. Wedding favors, attendants' gifts, and other personalized paraphernalia can be ordered online and shipped directly to the wedding venue. Just be sure you leave plenty of time for shipping delays—you can never tell when the postal workers in a country may decide to strike or declare a national holiday. Have every item clearly marked to be held for the bride by name and her arrival date. Keep in touch with the wedding coordinator to be sure that deliveries arrive.

The most important cargo to be transported—other than the bride and groom—is the wedding dress. The surest way to get it there is to carry it on the plane yourself. Your bridal shop will pack it in a hanging bag, and the airlines can usually find room in the first-class closet for a wedding dress, even if the bride travels in coach.

Ship the dress if you must but . . . one bride sent her wedding dress to Hawaii, it arrived ahead of her, and the hotel sent it back. The dress made its second trip to Hawaii just a day before the wedding. It arrived in time, but the bride was a basket case.

Rehearse hair at home. Few brides can afford to import their hairstylists or makeup artists to their destination weddings. The next best thing is to consult with your local beauty gurus, have them do a test of the wedding hairdo and makeup, and take lots of pictures. It is much simpler for a strange stylist to copy a hairdo than to try to figure out what the bride has in mind. Some makeup artists will give you diagrams and step-by-step directions so that you and the bride can re-create the effect yourselves.

Sing in the rain. As the mother of the bride, you want the wedding to go off without a hitch. But one person's wedding mishap is another's sweetest memory. When a spectacular wedding reception on a rooftop in the Caribbean was disrupted by a tropical deluge, the mother of the bride went ballistic. While she ranted and railed, the bride and groom danced in the rain and loved every moment of it.

Reality Check #10

QUESTIONS TO ASK BEFORE THE BRIDE AND GROOM BOOK THEIR OFF-THE-BEATEN-TRACK DREAM WEDDING

1. Are they planning to go to Paradise in hurricane, typhoon, earthquake, or tsunami season?

2. Have there been any recent outbreaks of Ebola, *E. coli,* or any other interesting diseases?

3. Does travel to the wedding venue involve trains, planes, automobiles, dogsleds, canoes, camels, burros, water buffalo, or yaks?

4. How close to the wedding venue is the nearest bathroom? hospital? Starbucks?

5. How likely are the wedding guests to encounter anti-American demonstations, Greenpeace protests, civil war, or strikes by air-traffic controllers, garbage collectors, and so on?

6. Has *Survivor* recently filmed at this location?

7. Is the wedding menu going to include such local delicacies as deep-fried beetles, sheep's eyes, or reindeer tongue?

8. Before the bride and groom leave home, does the U.S. government advise them to have:

   a. Bottled water
   b. A first-aid kit
   c. Innoculations
   d. A will

11

IT'S A DATE

"Have you set a date?" That's the first question everyone asks the engaged couple and the mother of the bride. It sounds like a simple question. You may think that all you have to do is find a location, find out when it is available, check the schedules of the main actors in the drama, then book the best available date in the season your daughter wants to be wed.

Before you get that far, you better look at a calendar. And not just any calendar. Check one that includes holidays, days that are celebrated so universally that they ought

to be holidays, and dates that could doom the marriage before it starts.

A bride determined to marry in the winter was pleased to discover that her chosen venue had an opening for a Saturday night in January. It also happened to be Super Bowl weekend. The couple got married in February instead.

There are fewer weddings on Super Bowl weekend than any other weekend of the year, according to weddingchannel.com. Brides who make their grooms choose between them and the big game may get the guy to the altar, but they won't keep them for long. At one New York wedding on Super Bowl Sunday, all the men deserted immediately after the ceremony. "Every man was downstairs at the bar, watching the game, and I couldn't seduce them back," reported the harried wedding planner.

Whether the groom's team won or lost, the bride was the biggest loser.

Depending on who you are and where you are, there may be other dates that should be avoided at all costs. Schedule a wedding on the weekend before a presidential election in Washington, D.C., and the guests will be polling each other when they should be toasting the happy couple. Plan a celebration for a family of Scots on Robert Burns's birthday and you'll have to serve haggis to men in skirts.

Some dates are so tied to sorrow that they'll cast a pall over the celebration. September 11 is a prime example. Some dates are so linked to family celebrations that guests will be reluctant to leave home for them. Thanksgiving week and Christmas week come to mind.

You'll want to check for religious holidays—even if you don't celebrate them, some of your guests probably do. If basketball, baseball, football, or World Cup soccer is the groom's religion, check those schedules, too.

Long holiday weekends have pluses and minuses. It is easier for the wedding party and guests to travel without missing work for wedding events. On the other hand, they'll have a harder time getting flights, and they probably won't be able to use frequent flier miles. Also, since people make long-range plans for three-day weekends, they'll need even more notice of your daughter's wedding.

In some cities, weeknight weddings are

popular—the costs are lower and Jewish couples don't have to worry about interfering with the Sabbath. Thursdays are popular in summer in New York society circles because they don't interfere with weekends at the Hamptons. TV news reporter George Stephanopoulos and Ali Wentworth got married on a Tuesday. That worked for them since Stephanopoulos works weekends. If almost all of the guests are local and nobody wants to celebrate into the wee hours, a midweek wedding works well. For out-of-towners, it is a huge hassle.

May and June are still the most popular months for weddings, although September and October are moving up fast. If the bride and groom want to marry at the height of the wedding season, they'll either have to start planning earlier or be more flexible about where they get married.

Coincidentally, May, June, September, and October are also the height of the allergy season. Before you plan an outdoor wedding, you might want to check the groom's medical history. Some guests might take his watery eyes and wheezing as a sign that he's less than thrilled about getting married.

If your guest list is far beyond what your venue or your budget can handle, you may want to discourage a lot of out-of-town relatives—particularly those related to the groom—from coming to the wedding. Under these circumstances, don't even think about a wedding in autumn in New York, in February in Florida, in Washington, D.C., during cherry blossom season, or in San Francisco at any time of year.

Okay, you've checked all of these dates and, miracle of miracles, found one that doesn't conflict with the bride's, the groom's, or the immediate families' schedules, religions, or athletic allegiances. You've booked the preacher and the venue. Whom do you tell and how do you tell them?

Your daughter will want to send a save-the-date card. This is kind of an pre-invitation invitation, telling prospective guests when and where the wedding will take place. There is a tendency to get cute with save-the-date cards—sending a piece of rope with the message "We're getting hitched" or a "Lucky in love" scratch-off card with the date hidden under the hearts. Some couples send refrigerator magnets, which will take their place among the kids' art and dentist appointment cards.

There is one problem with save-the-date cards—they commit you to inviting people way before you would otherwise narrow down the guest list. Send the card out six months in advance and, by the time the wedding rolls around, the bride may not be speaking to some of those people. But it's too late—they've saved the date.

The people closest to the bride and groom, the ones they really want at the wedding, know the date long before they get a card announcing it. The bride, the groom, and both families call or e-mail their nearest and dearest with the news.

If you send Christmas or holiday cards every year, you can add a note about the wedding to those people you really want to attend. We asked close friends and family to decorate a fabric square for Meredith's wedding canopy. At the bottom of the sheet of directions for decorating the square, we asked people to save the date.

If your daughter insists on sending out save-the-date cards, keep them simple and keep down the number of people who get them. Or talk her into something sensible like a save-the-date toenail clipper, beer opener, or eyeglass case.

Reality Check #11

REASONS TO RETHINK THE WEDDING DATE

1. It's the bride's anniversary with her ex.

2. It's the groom's anniversary with his ex.

3. It's your anniversary with your ex.

4. It's the start of duck, deer, or bargain hunting season.

5. It's the start of your city's cherry blossom, apple blossom, orange blossom, peach, magnolia, avocado, okra, strawberry, blueberry, clam, crab, or crawdad festival.

6. The astrologer says the bride's moon is in the wrong house.

7. It's the day the bride's baby is due.

Part 3

THE WEDDING VENDORS

TELL IT TO THE JUDGE

"We are gathered here today in the sight of [insert God, if appropriate] to join this man and this woman in [insert Holy, if appropriate] matrimony."

Yes, but who is going to do the uniting?

Many marriages get off to a shaky start because the person doing the marrying says or does something that shocks, offends, incenses, or otherwise unsettles one family or the other. We may be ecumenicals on the outside, but ethnic and religious roots are buried deep. Weddings inspire families to invoke religious and ethnic traditions they abandoned or never embraced in the first place. Even weddings between coreligionists can be problematic. High church or low church? Greek Orthodox or Russian Orthodox? Reformed Jewish or Conservative Jewish?

Considering the perilous possibilities, there ought to be an oath for officiants similar to the Hippocratic Oath physicians take, to "abstain from whatever is deleterious and mischievous."

Of course, one person's mischief is another person's mantra.

I thought I had the officiant thing down pat. My daughter, a nice Jewish girl, was marrying a nice Jewish boy. We belong to a congregation, albeit an unconventional one. Founded by aging hippies and free spirits in Washington, D.C., our congregation doesn't have a building or an affiliation with any organized branch of Judaism. All celebrations are vegetarian, we evoke "Sarah, Rebecca, Rachel, and Leah" along with "Abraham, Isaac, and Jacob," and if you'd rather save the whales than the Israelis, that's just fine with us.

So I called Rabbi David to sign him up for Meredith's wedding. "Congratulations," he said. He'll put the June date on his calendar. But there was one little problem. Meredith was getting married on Saturday, June 21, the longest day of the year. Saturday is the Sabbath. Traditionally, a Jewish wedding cannot take place until sundown, the end of the Sabbath. In June, the sun doesn't set until nearly 9 o'clock.

Our free-thinking officiant wasn't so free as to violate this age-old tradition.

Generations of June brides have solved this problem by holding a cocktail reception before the ceremony. While the bride cooled her heels in a holding room, the guests often proceeded to drink, drink, and be merry. At my cousin Judy's July wedding, my father disappeared for hours. We finally found him asleep in the backseat of a car in the parking lot. He missed the ceremony, the dinner, and the Viennese dessert table. While the bride was throwing her bouquet, he was throwing up in the bushes.

There had to be another way, I thought. Surely there was a rabbi somewhere who was willing to interpret religious law more broadly. I called Rabbi Harold White, Jewish chaplain at Georgetown University and a frequent officiant at mixed marriages.

He had no problem with sundown, but he had a big problem with June. He leaves for Nantucket as soon as spring semester finishes. He referred me to another rabbi who teaches law at another university.

The lawyer rabbi was from a more pragmatic sect. He said, in effect, "When would you like sundown to be?" We agreed on 7:00 p.m.

I was comfortable with that. After all, it was certain to be sundown somewhere on the planet.

I called Rabbi David to say that I was truly sorry, and I respected his principles, but we couldn't wait until 9:00 p.m. to start the wedding. Meredith was being married in a parks department facility that required that we be out of the building by midnight.

A few days later, Rabbi David called back with a truly inspired solution. Religious law forbids the conduct of business on the Sabbath. What if we conducted the "business"

of the wedding before and after the Sabbath? Meredith and Tony could sign their marriage contract on Friday before sundown. We could hold the ceremony during daylight on Saturday and the couple could exchange vows and rings. The only other "work"—the groom stepping on the symbolic glass and shattering it—would wait until after sunset.

Meredith loved the idea. Tony loved the idea.

Rabbi David had found a way to marry tradition with practicality. Since then, several brides have adopted the Meredith solution. It brings a tear to my eye to think of all the guests at future Jewish summer weddings who will be spared the agony of the endless midsummer cocktail hour.

We weren't the only ones to find a compromise between respect for ritual and respect for the sensibilities of the bride, the groom, and the wedding guests. One

Catholic couple held their lengthy nuptial mass on the Saturday night before their public wedding, with only close family in attendance. They had a short marriage ceremony and the reception for all of their friends and family on Sunday.

Traditional Indian weddings can last for two or three days. A bride and groom whose parents were all devout Hindus found an accommodating Hindu priest who was willing to perform their ceremony in 45 breakneck minutes.

It can be a challenge to find an officiant whose very presence will infuse the wedding with a spirit of joy and meet the needs of all of the parties. If you are an active member of a church, temple, synagogue, or mosque, your daughter is getting married in your hometown, and she is marrying someone of the same branch of the same faith, you are truly blessed. You just call your priest, rabbi, minister, imam, or other spiritual leader and reserve the date.

If your daughter has chosen a popular wedding month—September and October are just as popular as May and June now—you'll want to put in your request posthaste. Remember, you're competing not only with other weddings but also—according to your theology—with confirmations, christenings, and bar mitzvahs. You also need to allow time for the officiant to get to know the groom and to schedule the premarriage counseling that many clergy require the couple to attend. If the only religion involved in the wedding is "none of the above," you need only find a willing and available judge, justice of the peace, or clerk in city hall to perform the ceremony. Either way, you can skip this chapter.

However, if you are one of the unaffiliated, uninitiated, or uncertain or if the bride and groom come from different religious or cultural traditions, read on!

Admit it! You always thought—and secretly hoped—that your daughter would marry in the culture and faith of her forefathers.

It is a sentiment that knows no boundaries. It may be hard to picture, but audiences in Japan love *Fiddler on the Roof.* As the fictional Tevye shakes his head at daughters who ignore tradition and take their lives in their own hands, you can hear okansans and otosans murmuring "ah so." The father in *My Big Fat Greek Wedding* is Tevye's spiritual son. A fat lot of good it did him, you may recall.

Intermarriage is a fact of life. A recent survey conducted by United Jewish Communities found that the rates of intermarriage are rising. Before 1970, 13 percent of Jews married outside the faith. By the year 2000, 47 percent of Jews married non-Jews. Catholics, Protestants, Muslims, and Hindus are seeing similar patterns.

The huge increase in international travel and study abroad—not to mention the Internet—have widened the romantic possibilities. The children we raised to embrace people of every race, religion, and national origin have taken us at our word.

The result can be uncomfortable for even the most liberal parents. As one New York mother whose son was about to marry a girl from New Delhi put it, "Sure, we offered him the world, but we didn't expect him to take it."

You may think you are handling your daughter's nuptial diversity well. But finding an officiant, deciding where to hold the ceremony, and helping to script the ceremony itself will be the true tests.

There are several books and Web sites that offer examples of readings and rituals for interfaith wedding ceremonies that incorporate both families' traditions. For example, *Joining Hands and Hearts: Interfaith, Intercultural Wedding Celebrations,* by Reverend Susanna Stefanachi Macomb, offers ideas on crafting the wedding ceremony. An online shop called Interfaith Wedding Mall (www.interfaithweddingmall.com) offers products to represent Judaism, Islam, Buddhism, Hinduism, Christianity, Baha'i, Zoroastrian, Sikh, Shinto, and other faiths. The Web site weddingofficiants.com can provide names of preachers, pastors, priests, rabbis, celebrants, and so on, who perform interfaith marriages.

Since most major religions share a belief in one supreme being, there are many prayers and sentiments that can be shared. You can ask the officiant or officiants to refer to God in a universal way rather than invoking Jesus, Yahweh, Allah, or Buddha—or to skip God altogether. It also helps if you pick a neutral setting—a hotel, historic house, nondenominational university chapel, or your own backyard—so that neither family feels slighted.

Choose your officiant wisely, and no one will feel they have wandered into the wrong pew. Here are some possible solutions.

The Side-by-Side Solution. The easiest way to accommodate two traditions is to employ two officiants. According to *Celebrating Interfaith Marriages,* by Rabbi Devon A. Lerner, there are clergy in almost every denomination and community who are willing to participate in an interfaith ceremony. Catholic priests, for example, " . . . are obligated by church law to do everything in their power to promote healthy marriages, which includes the blessing of and participation in interfaith marriages," Lerner writes.

That doesn't mean every priest, rabbi, minister, or imam will take part in marrying people of different faiths. You may have to ask around, call liberal congregations, and seek out national groups. One such group is the Rabbinic Center for Research and Counseling (908-233-0419), which publishes a nationwide list of rabbis who conduct interfaith weddings.

Be sure that both officiants are on the same page of the wedding program. At one Catholic-Jewish wedding, the priest assured the couple that he would not invoke the Trinity. But at the ceremony itself, he managed to sneak in the Father, the Son, and the Holy Ghost. Lightning did not strike the Jewish side of the aisle, but there were a few uncomfortable moments.

The Separate-but-Equal Solution. Who says that a couple can only get married once? Sometimes the easiest way to respect two cultures is to hold two wedding cere-monies. And few brides will object to the idea of two wedding dresses. The bride can wear her Chinese red cheongsam for a traditional Buddhist ceremony or her scarlet sari for the Hindu ceremony and then change into creamy white for the Christian or Jewish ceremony. The rites can be conducted in the language of the faith, be it Greek, Russian, or Urdu, and no one will feel that their heritage was watered down for popular consumption.

One Maryland couple had a traditional Christian ceremony on the back porch of the Baltimore Museum of Industry, overlooking the harbor. Then everyone went inside for a Rod Nam Sung, a Thai ceremony. The two mothers placed flower garlands around the couples' necks, and the groom's father crowned them with connected wreaths made of twine.

The Interfaith-Minister Solution. An interfaith contemplative minister is one "who respects all paths leading toward a deepening of a person's relationship with the divine, and who upholds the sanctity and oneness of creation." The bride and groom can design the ceremony with the minister, selecting readings and prayers from a wide range of spiritual traditions. (For more information, call the Interfaith Theological Seminary in Tucson, Arizona, at 520-256-1883.) If your daughter and her beloved want to meditate, cogitate, or levitate, they can do so with appropriate blessings.

The Tell-It-to-the-Judge Solution. One way to keep everything civil is to have a civil ceremony. Having a judge do the marrying doesn't mean the ceremony has been relegated to a faceless bureaucrat or a dusty corner in the county courthouse. Supreme Court Justice Ruth Bader Ginsburg has performed weddings for several of her former clerks. A federal court of appeals judge from Boston recently married a couple on the beach in Georgetown, Maine. Even a barefoot judge can make a union legal!

However, in some states, judges cannot do the marrying. In North Carolina, only a magistrate can perform a marriage ceremony. Magistrates are forbidden, by law, to charge more than $20 for this service. So it is not surprising that they don't relish the prospect of traveling far from the county clerk's office or spending their nights and weekends presiding at weddings.

One couple discovered that their weekend request would be posted in the clerk's office for selection by one of the magistrates. How often did a request like this get "selected," the bride-to-be inquired. "Almost never," the clerk replied. The bride's family had visions of hosting a giant cocktail party with no wedding ceremony. Finally, the bride's father was able to call in a favor and get someone who knew someone else to get a magistrate to officiate.

The Ordain-Your-Own Solution. Online ordination can enable a friend or relative to perform the wedding ceremony. There are several "churches" that can make a near and dear one a member of the clergy, including the Universal Life Church (www.ulc.net), Universal Ministries (www.universalministeries.com), and the Spirit Gathering, Ordination "according to the Order of Melchizedek" (www.spiritgathering.com).

Are these ordinations legal? Absolutely. In 1974, the U.S. government was sued by the Universal Life Church—and the church won. The U.S. District Court for the Eastern District of California likened Web ordination to "mass conversions of a typical revival or religious crusade." Despite this comparison, you needn't worry that the officiant you select will speak in tongues or require all present to repent . . . unless you want her to, of course.

Most Internet faiths espouse beliefs that are universal. Your instant minister can design the marriage service with the bride and groom to suit everybody's theological needs.

The Officiant-for-a-Day Solution. In some states, a friend or relative can apply to the state or local government for permission to officiate at a wedding. Sometimes the officiant even gets a title, like deputy marriage commissioner, with the understanding that the title is good for one day or one wedding only.

In some states, Colorado, for example, you don't even need official permission to be dubbed an officiant. As long as the couple has a marriage license, anyone can do the honors. In Pennsylvania, where the Quaker tradition is still strong, the gathering of family and friends who witness the vows is all the "officiant" the couple needs.

Reality Check # 12

WORDS TO WED BY

No matter who the officiant is, there is a good chance that the couple will choose to write their own vows, eschewing the old "honor and obey, "in sickness and in health," and so on, in favor of pledging back rubs and shared bank accounts. They will often include readings of a nonscriptural nature including but not limited to selections from the gospel according to Dr. Seuss. If so, you can remind the lovebirds that it is not necessary to read the entire volume of these beloved classics. A little bit of *Hop on Pop* goes a long way.

LET 'EM EAT CAKE

All I wanted at my wedding was champagne and wedding cake. The banquet manager of the Plaza Hotel, the aptly named Peter Herring, quickly disabused me of that notion. "You could invite your relatives for a wedding held at 3 o'clock in the morning and they'd still expect a full-course, sit-down dinner," he said.

Alas, he was right. What did he mean by "your relatives," you ask? Anyone with an ounce of ethnic blood, regardless of ethnicity, would qualify. Our people—and that includes 99 percent of the world—expect to be fed at celebrations. That doesn't mean a nosh or a nibble. It means a groaning board.

Even the upper crust rarely has the crust to serve only a bit of the bubbly and a few finger sandwiches. Besides, as noted previously, guests tend to get surly and sloshed when they aren't fed—a situation to be avoided at all costs.

For her wedding, Meredith wanted more than champagne and wedding cake. She wanted a sit-down dinner—but with certain restrictions. No red meat. No endangered fish—Chilean sea bass have been "overfished" and could not be on the menu, she informed me.

Tony had only one stipulation—he wanted food that he recognized.

I, on the other hand, had lots of opinions on this subject. Part of my job for the past 17 years has been overseeing special events for *Washingtonian* magazine. I've learned a few tricks along the way:

‣ If you serve wonderful, plentiful hors d'oeuvres during the cocktail hour, you can skip the appetizer at dinner.

‣ Starving guests can attack a buffet table like locusts, leaving the timid or well mannered with nothing to eat but the garnish. Passed hors d'oeuvres served by waiters give everyone a fighting chance at the food.

‣ You can't expect white-glove manners when it comes to food. Many guests act as if they haven't eaten in months and have no idea where their next meal is coming from. At one wedding, the bride, whose father and uncle own a number of McDonald's in the New York area, surprised guests by serving hamburgers, cheeseburgers, and Chicken McNuggets during the cocktail hour, along with the usual wedding fare.

"As soon as they filled the serving trays, guests cleaned them out," the bride reported. "One of our guests stuffed his pockets and every once in a while, during the reception, you'd find him munching on a hamburger."

‣ *Washingtonian*'s publisher Phil Merrill has a "one-bite rule" for hors d'oeuvres. You should be able to pick it up and eat it in one bite without any mess left on your hands. The first corollary to the "one-bite rule" is that cocktail shrimp are served without tails and no one is ever left holding a skewer stick, desperately seeking a place to deposit it. The second corollary is to be selective with the sauces. If you serve anything with sauce at a standup party, every third man will spill it on his tie.

‣ Preset the salad course. That lessens the amount of time waiters have to spend serving and increases the time your guests can dance, drink, and be merry.

Caterers can accommodate special diets—within reason. Party vendors always have a few vegetarian entrées on hand. With advance notice, nonkosher caterers can make arrangements to provide kosher meals. However, it is impossible to meet the food needs of every vegan, low-carb dieter, or raw food enthusiast. This is a wedding, not a restaurant. There will always be some food the guest can eat, even if he or she can't eat everything that is served.

Pick your splurges. We went for a full bar with premium brands of liquor and beer. But, when it came time to toast the newlyweds, I requested that the waiters offer champagne to all guests but only pour it for those who said "yes." Some people don't drink at all. Some hate champagne. Some have already left the party.

For dessert—let 'em eat cake. If the wedding cake is delicious, you don't need another dessert. Working on *Washingtonian*'s wedding section, I tasted 40 wedding cakes. Many of the most beautiful cakes turned out to be the worst-tasting. The most elaborate wedding cakes are covered in rolled fondant, a supersweet chewy sugar paste that can be sculpted into intricate designs. Many people find the taste of fondant as appealing as wallpaper paste.

Cakes with ambitious, unusual fillings and flavors often sound better than they taste. A tiramisù cake or a spice cake will appeal to a smaller number of people than chocolate mousse or strawberry shortcake.

Also, you don't need a gargantuan wedding cake. At many weddings, the caterer bakes two cakes—a modest wedding cake for show and a large sheet cake in the same flavor to feed the majority of the guests.

When we were planning Meredith's wedding, I developed a set of specs—number of guests, number of courses, alcohol requirements—and sent them to several caterers. That's when I discovered that the cost of the actual food might be reasonable, but food was only a small part of the bill. We had to pay for linens, dishes, glasses, flatware, bartenders, and servers.

"Wouldn't it be cheaper just to send everybody to Bermuda for a week?" Benjamin asked.

It was a close call. However, by eliminating the appetizer, an extra dessert, and a midnight snack for guests, we were able to make our catering budget work.

Another surprise was the scornful treatment I got from some caterers when I questioned costs. I know that June is a busy month for party vendors, and ours wasn't the biggest event of the season. But what was I, chopped liver? In fact, judging from the tone of voice of some of the caterers I called, I was lower than chopped liver. I was liverwurst.

The quality of the service is as important as the quality of the food at a wedding. Lots of caterers could have satisfied our guests' appetites, but I wanted a caterer who wanted the job and was willing to work with us. Our final choice was a lovely lady named Cynthia in Alexandria, Virginia. She liked us, she really liked us. Or, at the very least, she acted like she liked us.

After we picked our caterer, we still had lots of decisions to make. There were dozens of possibilities for every course. Crab puffs or cheese puffs? Florentine or en croûte? Polenta or pilaf? Meredith and Tony were asked to narrow their choices to a handful of selections in each category and then all of us would go to a tasting before deciding on the final menu.

Everything on a caterer's menu sounds delicious. The descriptions alone are pure poetry. One caterer suggested that our main course should be pheasant with dried fresh fruits accompanied by a complex crackled pepper sauce. This would be accompanied by mixed black grains—"a stunning combination of black barley, black rice, wild rice, black quinoa, and beluga lentils tossed with shaved scallions—and sautéed artichokes, fava beans, and roasted Peruvian purple potatoes."

Complex crackled pepper sauce—as opposed to simple crackled pepper sauce? Black grains? Fava beans?

Another caterer proposed an hors d'oeuvre of chicken, prosciutto, and sage spiedini with roasted red pepper rouille. Recognizing that some of us Philistines might not be able to figure out exactly what she was talking about, she explained that, to create this delicacy, morsels of boneless and skinless chicken breast were marinated in fresh herbs, garlic, and lemon. Then these morsels were skewered, wrapped in prosciutto and sage, and grilled. The skewers were served with sweet red pepper rouille. My French-English dictionary defines "rouille" as "rust." We opted to steer clear of decomposing metals.

The father of the bride and the groom cannot understand why they can't get food they know and love. I have seen grown men cry when, after much begging and pleading, a caterer, sniffing with disgust, agrees to serve pigs-in-blankets during the cocktail hour.

Snob appeal is a big factor in wedding menus. At home she may eat Cool Whip, but at the wedding, the bride demands crème fraîche. Caterers understand this. The menus we saw offered hominy soufflé, potato flan with chives, tenderloin noisettes, and grilled slices of Magret duck.

Amazingly, some of the snootiest-sounding dishes have the most humble origins. Hominy soufflé is the tarted-up cousin of down-home grits.

Some brides hedge their bets, offering guests a choice of two entrées or the ever-popular "surf 'n' turf." Personally, I wish they would make up their minds and serve a healthy portion of something wonderful rather than a child-size serving of two entrées that have no business being on the same plate. Somehow, the fish sauce always merges with the beef gravy, creating the gastronomic equivalent of sludge.

Reverse snobbery is the newest wedding trend. Some brides are serving Big Macs and Egg McMuffins instead of fillets and soufflés. Actress Julia Roberts invited guests to her New Mexico ranch for hot dogs and corn on the cob. At another wedding, the gourmet entree was followed by ice cream cones for dessert.

When it came time for our tasting, neither the groom nor the father of the bride were able to attend. (I swear this was not deliberate.) Meredith, her maid of honor, Claire, Tony's parents, Susan and Andy Goldstein, and I did the tasting.

First, we feasted on lots of different hors d'oeuvres. This was especially important to me because, given my druthers, I would fill up on hors d'oeuvres and then go straight to dessert, skipping the entrée altogether. Eventually we chose Maryland lump crab cakes served with rémoulade dipping sauce, coconut-encrusted shrimp with persimmon dipping sauce, smoked buffalo mozzarella and roasted peppers on a crouton with basil chiffonade, walnut brie tarts, and sliced steak on brioche. By serving sauces, I was violating a *Washingtonian* party rule, but I decided to let all of the men in ties fend for themselves.

Tony loves shrimp, Meredith loves cheese, and Marylanders feel an obligation to offer crab cakes. The sliced steak was for Benjamin. At the wedding he never actually got to eat any steak, but afterward he did say that it looked delicious on the video.

For the salad course, Cynthia suggested a veritable vegetable work of art—a lettuce bouquet in a cucumber vase with a goat cheese medallion, caramelized walnuts, and raspberries. I've never known quite how to attack a vertical salad—knocking it over seems like an insult to the creator. Cynthia urged us to topple at will.

Now for the main course. By this time, we had eliminated salmon (too ordinary), turkey (too Thanksgiving), duck (too fatty), squab (too bony), and any of the other suggested fish dishes (too many people dislike fish). That left chicken and . . . chicken. Fortunately, caterers are ingenious in creating new and novel ways to serve chicken.

Given three versions of chicken with impressive ingredients and paragraph-long descriptions, the winner was . . . chicken. We liked the one with the cornmeal and coriander crust with black bean mango salsa, three-pepper slaw with chipotle dressing, and vegetables. It wasn't the most elegant, but it tasted the best.

Many couples save their flights of fancy for the wedding cake. I've seen cakes decorated to match the lace on the wedding dress or dyed to match the flowers. A shoe-loving bride commissioned a $3,000 cake that looked like stacked Manolo Blahnik, Charles Jourdan, and Ferragamo shoe boxes. It was topped by a spun-sugar sling back. Another bride requested a cake topped with miniature Vuitton luggage—edible, of course.

There is a Washington-area cake baker who specializes in sugar paintings. One cake had paintings of scenes of an English cottage garden in gilded frames.

One cake wasn't enough for a Los Angeles bride and groom. They had 16—one for each table. Each was shaped like a beloved object—there was a champagne bucket, a photo album, and a crazy hat. Sadly, there wasn't a Blahnik in the bunch—but they probably couldn't afford it anyway. A custom cake can cost as much as $10 a slice.

At the other extreme, some couples are choosing artistic arrangements of cupcakes or Krispy Kreme doughnuts. In her heyday, Martha Stewart featured just such a "cake" on the cover of *Martha Stewart Weddings*. The cupcakes weren't just piled up, of course. They were iced in aqua, stacked in tiers, and topped with monogrammed fondant hearts.

Meredith and Tony just wanted a cake that tasted good—and had no liquor in it. For God's sake, people, why mess up a good cake?

The one we chose was white chocolate cake with fresh strawberries, white chocolate mousse, and white chocolate buttercream frosting. The design was a simple basket weave pattern, and the cake was topped with the same bride and groom Tony's grandparents had on their wedding cake more than 60 years ago.

After the wedding, Cynthia gave me a broiler pan filled with leftover cake. Susan Goldstein and I took it into the hotel bar and sat there eating away. True, we didn't bother with plates, but we did use forks. We weren't totally shameless.

Reality Check #13

DO YOU NEED A GROOM'S CAKE AS WELL AS A WEDDING CAKE?

The groom's cake is a Southern tradition that has crept like kudzu into weddings everywhere. According to wedding lore, the groom's cake was a gift from the bride, a symbol of their sweet life together. It was a dark, liquor-soaked fruitcake, cut into squares, placed in monogrammed boxes, and given to the guests as favors. A more ingenious way of getting rid of Christmas fruitcake has yet to be devised!

Also according to legend, a single woman who placed a piece of the groom's cake under her pillow would dream of her future husband. This was an ingenious way of getting guests to actually *accept* the box, once they realized there was fruitcake inside.

These days the cake can be chocolate, red velvet, or any other flavor the groom fancies. It is often shaped like an object of the groom's affection—other than the bride, of course. There have been grooms' cakes resembling police badges, bass fish, baseball bats, boats, golf clubs, computers, briefcases, and beer bottles. One bride re-created the Leaning Tower of Pisa. The movie *Steel Magnolias* immortalized the armadillo cake.

Some wedding planners see the groom's cake as an alternative dessert, particularly when the parties cannot agree on a wedding cake flavor.

A happier trend is to serve the groom's cake at the rehearsal dinner. Since this is the wedding event most often hosted by the groom's family, I applaud this concept.

Let his mother re-create the red-velvet armadillo!

14

SMILE, YOU'RE ON CANDID CAMERA

Here's the most important thing you need to know about wedding pictures: Book the best photographer you can afford as soon as you set the date. The wedding music will fade, the flowers will die, and you won't even remember *if* you ate, let alone *what* you ate, at the reception. But the wedding pictures last forever.

We waited to line up a photographer, following the time line in the wedding guides. The standard advice is that you need to book a photographer six to eight months ahead. That's too late! We were just extraordinarily lucky that one of Wash-

ington's best wedding photographers was able to move his schedule around so that he could shoot Meredith's wedding. I only had to bump off one bar mitzvah boy to make it happen.

Why do you need to act so early? A caterer can cater several events the same day, a florist can make more than one bridal bouquet, but short of cloning, a photographer can only shoot one event at a time.

Now that every Dick and Jane seems to have a digital camera, it is easy to underestimate the importance of having a professional photographer. Sure, anybody can take wedding pictures. If they shoot enough of them, there are bound to be a few good ones. But only a pro can light pictures to make everyone look good.

Lots of brides place disposable cameras on the tables at the reception and urge guests to take their best shots. Afterward, the mother of the bride collects the cameras and develops the pictures. The results are usually a mixed bag of cute candids, out-of-focus close-ups, and pictures you wish you hadn't printed. At one wedding, a few friends of the groom took the cameras into the men's room for a series of unusual self-portraits. The groom swears he couldn't identify them from the pictures.

Wedding photography hasn't been the same since Jacqueline Bouvier married John F. Kennedy. Ms. Bouvier had been a newspaper photographer. While she cer-tainly sat for formal wedding portraits, she hired a photojournalist to shoot the actual wedding.

Today's brides can choose between two schools of wedding photographers. Traditional photographers specialize in posed pictures; photojournalists specialize in unposed "capture-the-moment" pictures, often shot in black-and-white.

Traditional photographers are often front and center. Photojournalists are more likely to fade into the background. Traditional photographers stop the newlyweds midpivot during the first dance so that they can face the camera and smile. Photojournalists show the blur as her skirt billows.

The Art of Wedding Photography, by Bambi Cantrell and Skip Cohen, is written for the professional photographer, but it offers a lot of useful information for the mother of the bride. Seen together, wedding photographs should, in the authors' words, "document the human experience and the personalities of two unique families coming together."

Denis Reggie, who took the wedding shot seen round the world of John F. Kennedy Jr. and Carolyn Bessette, is one of the new breed of wedding photographers. He is a photojournalist, an observer rather than a manipulator. Reggie was under orders to release only one wedding photo to the media. He shot the newlyweds as they were leaving the tiny church on Cumberland Island. Reggie swore that the couple was lost in their own love and blissfully unaware of his presence. Except for the flashbulbs popping in front of the faces of the most-photographed couple in the world, of course!

Reggie and other photojournalists believe that the most touching, evocative photographs of the wedding are often those that capture the small, magical moments that otherwise would be missed. For example, during the toasts, you'll be looking at the best man or the maid of honor. A photojournalist will also be looking at the bride and groom, capturing their reactions. Or following the grandmothers, who are always good for some great pictures.

Like many brides, Meredith wanted it all—great candids and great portraits. We looked at a lot of photographers' work—fortunately, many photographers have Web sites that display their pictures—before selecting one who combined both photo approaches. Our wedding photographer, Michael, also advised us to have a second shooter, to increase our chances of getting everything we wanted in both color and black-and-white.

A few weeks before the wedding, Michael met with Meredith and spoke to me about all of the shots we wanted. (We didn't want table pictures. We did ask for pictures of people important to us—but we forgot a few. Guests who didn't get up to dance or mingle aren't in the pictures. That's something we forgot about.)

You should also ask your religious leader how he or she feels about taking pictures and shooting video during the ceremony. That was not a problem for us.

Michael and I worked out a schedule for the day of the wedding—shooting time with the bride and groom, the wedding party, and the families. He needed at least an hour with the bride and groom alone. Meredith and Tony chose to do this before the wedding. The two of them not only saw each other beforehand but also rode together in the limo to the wedding site.

(But they didn't miss that "Oh my God, she's gorgeous" moment. I'll never forget my son-in-law's reaction when he saw Meredith in her bridal gown, gliding across the hotel lobby toward him. "That's an awesome dress. It's sleeveless," he said. And with that profound fashion commentary, they headed off to their wedding together.)

I know that seeing the bride on the wedding day is romantic sacrilege, but it gave Meredith and Tony time alone and plenty of time to work with the photographer without 200 eyes watching them.

Meanwhile, the limo went back to the hotel to pick up the wedding party. By the time the family pictures were done, the bride and groom were sequestered, separately, with their respective attendants.

I know other brides who've taken pictures before the wedding without breaking tradition. In some cases, the bride and groom are only photographed alone and with their respective families. One bride tried a novel approach. The groom was blindfolded or placed at an angle so that he wouldn't actually "see" the bride. Unfortunately, the camera could still see the blindfold.

After the bride and groom and wedding party shots, it was the families' turn to pose. How did I feel about standing still for the posed pictures? I was thrilled. Formal, posed pictures with flattering light give the mother of the bride a fighting chance to put her best face forward.

While photojournalism will capture the "heartbeat of the wedding," candid pictures are most flattering of the bride, the groom, and their contemporaries. During the festivities that followed, Michael caught Meredith and Tony enjoying themselves and each other. He also caught the mother of the bride at some unfortunate angles.

Take it from one who's seen sides of herself she's still trying to erase from memory, you want to take your time to smile for the camera. It helps to know how to pose.

A three-quarters view is likely to be more flattering than a straight-on picture. Bambi Cantrell has very specific advice for shooting flattering pictures: "Set [the subject's] feet a foot apart. Have her press her hips lightly back to accentuate the flattering S curve. You want to create body lines that flow rather than angle sharply."

Slightly bending both arms and legs makes you look more relaxed. If you are concerned about a double chin, ask the photographer to shoot from a slightly higher plane. Then pull your chest forward and lean slightly toward the camera, leading with your chin. Want to look 10 pounds thinner? Try the Oprah Winfrey trick. When she was photographed for the cover of *Vogue* magazine, Winfrey stood sideways and then twisted her torso so that her head was facing the camera.

Would this much attention to how you, the mother of the bride, look in the wedding pictures demonstrate an unnatural streak of vanity? Perhaps. But it is a far, far better thing to obsess about the pictures beforehand—when you can do something about how you look—than to agonize afterward when you look at the proofs.

Once you've given the photographer a list of people you definitely want photographed and posed for some pictures yourself, your work is done. The mother of the bride should not try to orchestrate or direct the photo session.

Yes, it's true that few young men are comfortable smiling for the camera. That's why you have hired a professional who is used to dealing with uncomfortable posers and reluctant smilers. He'll notice if the sun is reflecting on your husband's glasses. He knows how much energy you've expended creating the perfect setting, and he'll get into the room before the guests to shoot the tables, the centerpieces, and the cake. Relax.

If the bride doesn't want to be seen before the wedding, the photographer will need to whisk the couple and the wedding party away right after the ceremony. Don't rush the shooter—certainly not when he's taking a picture of you.

The wedding day isn't your one and only chance to get great wedding pictures. You can arrange in advance for your photographer to do another photo shoot at a scenic location. In Washington, D.C., couples often put on their wedding finery again to get pictures of themselves standing on the steps of the Lincoln Memorial, the Jefferson Memorial, or the Capitol, on the rooftop of the Kennedy Center overlooking the city, or above the waters of Great Falls on the Potomac River. (To shoot at one of the memorials, you need to call the National Park Service at 202-619-7225 for permission.)

In San Francisco, there are great pictures of newlyweds at Big Sur, in the Muir

Woods, or in the Japanese Tea Garden in Golden Gate Park. New Yorkers shoot pictures on the Staten Island Ferry with spectacular skylines behind them. One couple stopped between the church and the reception to shoot pictures in Grand Central Station.

Every city has landmarks and landscapes that can make great pictures. There's another advantage to these location shoots—since the wedding is over, the bride and groom are bound to be much more relaxed.

You could say that it was actress Grace Kelly who invented the wedding video in 1956. She was still under contract to MGM when she married Prince Rainier of Monaco. Kelly fulfilled her contract by letting MGM film the wedding. Brides have been behaving like movie stars ever since!

Here is all you need to know about wed-ding videos: You want one. Benjamin could not understand why we needed a videographer. We had a great photographer. Wouldn't that be enough coverage for one wedding? And who wants to sit and watch a wedding video, anyway?

Benjamin is now a believer. A wedding video doesn't just allow you to relive the wedding, it also allows you to see all of those wonderful moments you missed the first time.

We missed the wedding procession—we were in the back, with the bride. We couldn't see ourselves walking Meredith down the aisle or the tableau of the wedding party during the ceremony. During the reception, we were so busy working the room that we never saw Meredith and Tony cut the cake, our son, the groomsman, dancing with one of the bridesmaids, the groom dancing with all of the bridesmaids, or the tears in Meredith's eyes when Benjamin spoke—thank goodness, it was all captured on video.

There are two schools of videographers. Some act like Hollywood directors, trying to run the show. Others act like documentary purists, fading into the background so they don't become part of the story. Meredith asked our videographer to be "present" but not omnipresent. He captured everything—the video is more than 2 hours long. If I were a movie critic, I would say that it dragged in a few places but the leads were magnificent. A good part of a wedding is formulaic and sentimental. I say "a good part" advisedly. Meredith and Tony's wedding video starts by panning photos of their childhoods and their families as they grew. It ends with a montage of wedding moments. In all of the other videos I saw, the montages looked cheesy. But I've watched Meredith's montage over and over again and loved every gooey, mozzarella moment.

Who gets the wedding pictures and the wedding videos? That depends on the deal you make with your photographer and videographer.

Most of the time, despite the protestations from certain parents, the bride and groom get the big wedding album. Parents can order prints or ask for albums of their own, at an additional fee. Photographers often put the proofs on the Internet and let you order them directly. If grandparents or in-laws want pictures, you can direct them to the Web site.

Spare yourself the agony of the print order and prepare to wait. Some photographers take their own sweet time in getting prints to you. In the meantime, your friends can e-mail the digital photos they took, and some of the shots from the disposal cameras might miraculously be in focus and fit for mixed company.

Reality Check #14

WEDDING PICTURES NOBODY NEEDS TO SEE

1. The bride showing her adorable "just married" undies

2. The groom counting the wedding checks

3. Any man ogling a woman's décolletage

4. Any grandmother asleep at the table

5. Either the bride or the groom smashing the wedding cake into their beloved's face

6. The best man making out with the maid of honor in the bushes

7. The father of the bride sneaking a smoke in the bushes

8. Anyone relieving themselves in the bushes

15

DON'T THROW BOUQUETS AT ME

Roses are red and violets are blue until you start talking about wedding flowers. Suddenly, a rose can be citrus orange or jade green. Even a red rose can be either a preference rose or a black magic rose. Then there are all of the varieties of anemones, peonies, lilies, orchids, and species with syllables too numerous to mention. You may wonder if you're supposed to become an amateur botanist just to order the flowers.

What's more, each flower is more than the sum of its petals. There's a whole language of flowers, as any florist will tell you. A rose symbolizes true love. The bride can carry lilies of the valley as a sign of purity. Or it may be safer to stick to stephanotis as a symbol of happy marriage.

Flowers also go in and out of fashion. According to one report, the lowly carnation is making a comeback along with hand-tied nosegays, herbs and edibles bunched in with the flowers, and monochromatic bridal bouquets in vivid colors.

Wedding mavens estimate that almost 10 percent of the wedding budget goes for flowers. That figure can easily shoot skyward, the more elaborate and exotic the flowers get. While flowers in season—tulips in spring, asters in autumn—are the most economical, any flower the bride desires is growing somewhere in every season.

How do you decide how much flower power you need and who should supply it? First, set your petal priorities. Personal flowers count more than environmental flowers. The bridal bouquet, the bridesmaids' bouquets, and the boutonnieres will be in all the wedding pictures, so it pays to spend more on them.

Reception flowers count more than ceremony flowers. Most wedding ceremonies are blessedly short, and you really want the bride, not the floral arrangements, to shine. You can get away with a lot of greenery and skip most blooms altogether. Benjamin and I were married under a canopy of greens. It looks just fine in the very few wedding pictures where the canopy is even visible.

If there are other weddings in the same place on the same day, contact the mothers of those brides in advance. You may be able to share the cost of the ceremony flowers.

When it comes to reception flowers, table flowers count more than ambient room flowers. These are the flowers guests actually look at all evening. If they are looking at them too much, it means that the floral arrangements are so high that the guests cannot see each other.

If the room is attractive, you don't need to beribbon and begarland it just because it's a wedding. When you view the site, remember that the empty room will be filled with colorful tablecloths, centerpieces, dishes, food, and people.

A tent is a tent is a tent. You can hang crystal chandeliers, wrap the tent poles in garlands of roses, and call it Scheherazade, but it will still be a tent. Concentrate the flowers on the tables, not the tent.

Last, and indeed least, are the flowers for the cake table, the placecard table, and the powder rooms. These are nice touches, but most guests are too busy looking for their names or looking at their lipstick to notice.

Focus first on the bridal bouquet. Bridal bouquets have changed a lot over the years. The stiff cascades of white flowers have given way to colorful arrays carried by the arm-load, beauty-queen style, or packed in a tight bunch with the stems wrapped together with ribbon. Some bouquets include greens, berries, or feathers. Some are "composites" where the florist creates one giant rose from the petals of four dozen smaller roses.

Bridesmaids' bouquets don't have to match the bride's or each other's. Meredith's bridesmaids each carried a different variety of pink flowers. At another recent wedding, the maids all carried gerbera daisies in different colors.

The bouquets can do double duty. Meredith's bouquet served as the centerpiece on the "sweetheart" table. The bridesmaids' bouquets were placed around the wedding cake.

Mothers and grandmothers are usually "honored" with their own personal flowers. Many mothers carry small nosegays or one long-stemmed rose instead. This can get complicated and expensive when there are multiple biological and stepparents and grandparents.

We gave a corsage to the one grand-mother in attendance but skipped the rest. While the nosegay is one step ahead of a corsage, it seemed unnecessary to me. I already had my hands full. Of course, it's your daughter's party and if you feel that you need additional embellishment and it's okay with the bride, you can wear a rose in your teeth. Personally, I'd rather wear a dia-mond bracelet.

All the men in the family and in the wedding party get boutonnieres. Often the groom gets a different color or a different flower to distinguish him from the rest of the wedding party. While it is unlikely the bride would mistake him for the best man, a little extra insurance never hurts.

The groomsmen at Meredith's wedding had sprays of herbs instead of flowers. This worked better in theory than in practice. Most of the guests thought the groomsmen had lost their flowers on the way to the wedding.

Despite my protestations to the contrary, you *can* do your own flowers. There are online florists who will ship flowers and instructions for creating bouquets and centerpieces. For example, one wholesale package included 150 stems of light pink roses, 150 stems of medium pink roses, 150 stems of dark pink roses, five bunches of baby's breath, five bunches of leather fern, and 2 gallon bags of rose petals for $400. You'll have to supply the centerpiece containers, the floral clay, the ribbon, and any tools. You'll also have to deal with all those thorns!

Some brides opt for silk or beaded flowers—a much better idea for do-it-yourselfers. Fake flowers never have thorns and they can be arranged far in advance. They'll also last forever without any special effort.

Your daughter probably wants you to keep your hands off the flowers. Fortunately, there are lots of florists waiting to fulfill her every floral fantasy. How do you pick "the one"?

Florists make it easy. Many have Web sites and all have presentation books filled with pictures of centerpieces, bouquets, and room decorations they have done before. Most florists have a preferred style—fanciful, traditional, Asian, or modern.

Even after you identify a floral designer who shares your daughter's vision, you want to go to the first meeting armed with pictures the bride has clipped, showing bouquets and arrangements that she likes. A good florist should also ask a lot of questions about the bride's personal style, her color scheme, her dress, and the attendants' dresses. The florist should also see the sites and make suggestions about how he or she "sees" the wedding.

For Meredith's wedding, I suggested a florist whose work I had long admired. After Meredith looked at his Web site and liked his work, we set up a meeting at his studio. He and Meredith tiptoed through the tulips together—I was too worried about the guest list to think about flowers at the time. The two of them agreed on the bouquets for the wedding party. They chose two different centerpieces to alternate throughout the room. One used low, shallow bowls with floating candles wreathed in flowers. The other centerpiece was a grouping of three glass vases, each holding a different flower.

Nick supplied the bowls and vases from his inventory. The night of the wedding, I discovered that friends and relatives who wouldn't dream of walking out with a chair or a lamp have no qualms about marching off with a vase of flowers under the mistaken belief that if it's a centerpiece, it is up for grabs. I had to disabuse them of this notion.

They were welcome to carry off flowers but not the containers.

Reality Check #15

THE FINE POINTS OF FLOWER POWER

1. If you are old enough to remember wrist corsages, you are too old to wear one.

2. If you wear a shoulder corsage, you'll look like you're old enough to wear one.

3. No boutonniere should be big enough to look like a shoulder corsage.

4. Try to talk the bride out of a "toss" bouquet. Try to talk her out of tossing her bouquet, period. It is an archaic ritual dating from an era when embarrassing unmarried women was right up there with whoopee cushions as high comedy. It is so much nicer to present the bouquet to someone special—you, for instance.

THEY'RE PLAYING HER SONG

How important is music in the grand scheme of the wedding? The truth is that nothing matters less at the wedding ceremony and nothing matters more at the reception.

A wedding ceremony is primarily a visual experience. Sure the guests can look and listen at the same time—some can even chew gum while they do—but the background music fades as the pageantry grows. Whether it is a trio or quartet of classical musicians, an organist, or a disc jockey who plays appropriate selections while the wedding party comes down the aisle, the music is eminently forgettable.

The only exception is when a musician hits a sour note or the selection is so unusual that guests can't help but sit up and take notice. If the groom arrives at the altar to the tune of "Send in the Clowns," some may wonder if someone is trying to send a message.

But for the bride, the ceremony is more than sound. It is the sound track of her romantic dream. Others may scoff, but she'll read meaning into every note. She may spend weeks listening to Purcell's "Trumpet Tune" and "Bell Symphony" and Pachelbel's Canon in D Major, trying to decide which one best fits her journey to matrimony. She may wonder whether Vivaldi can segue into "Sunrise, Sunset." She may well agonize over whether a Jewish wedding can include Bach's "Jesu, Joy of Man's Desiring" since nary a word about Jesus is heard.

One Jewish mother of the bride could not bear the thought of "Jesu" appearing in the wedding program. The wedding planner solved the problem—the official name of the piece, "Largo" from Bach's Cantata #147, was the only name that appeared in print.

As mother of the bride, your job is to be both a music researcher and a sounding board. If the ceremony is being held in a house of worship, there may be limits on the ceremony music. You should check with the officiant before you and the bride finalize the musical selections. Some priests insist on sacred music. Some rabbis object to Wagner's Bridal Chorus, better known as "Here Comes the Bride," because of the composer's overt antisemitism.

However, as long as the officiant doesn't object, the bride and groom can march down the aisle to their own beat, be it "Linus and Lucy," the theme from Peanuts, Stevie Wonder's "You Are the Sunshine of My Life," or even something by the festively named Squirrel Nut Zippers.

My son-in-law picked "Ripple," by the Grateful Dead. When guests asked about the tune, I said that I believed it was an obscure selection from Handel's Water Music Suite.

If the church has an organist or other musicians on staff, it may be preferable to use the "house band" rather than to bring in outsiders. The site itself can also influence the ceremony music. It isn't enough to look at the place. You also have to check the acoustics. The string quartet that sounds lovely in a garden might get lost in a Gothic cathedral. The vaulted space may cry out for Bach and a thundering organ.

Few instruments convey the heavenly wedding feeling as well as a harp. But harps resonate best in small- or moderate-size spaces with stone or wooden walls. You can't set a harp down on the sand, on the ground, or on an uneven floor. Harpists won't pluck their strings in direct sunlight or next to the fireplace—the instrument is sensitive to temperature changes. And don't expect a harpist to cart the instrument up a hill, no matter how lovely the view is from the top.

Musical instruments must be cosseted and kept dry. That is why musicians operate on the Rolling Stone principle, "Gimme Shelter."

You'll want to have a contract with the booking agency or with the lead musician, spelling out who the players will be, where and when you need them to arrive, how long they will play, and what arrangements can be made for overtime.

The ceremony musicians usually start to play as soon as guests begin arriving, and they often continue to play through the cocktail reception. They'll dress formally or informally—you set the dress code. They can make suggestions or you can provide a playlist.

Once the bride and groom have done the "I dos," you are all ready to celebrate. Now music takes center stage.

You can't beat a band, according to Virginia wedding planner GiGi Lantz. Live musicians give an energy to a reception that no deejay can match, Lantz believes.

Every city has talent agencies that represent local bands. You can get videotapes or CDs to narrow down your choices, but you, the bride, and the groom will want to see the group in action before you book them.

How wide is their repertoire? A specialty band limits you to one kind of music. At one wedding, the bride wanted a swing band and the mother of the bride wanted klezmer music. They had two separate but equal bands in two different locations—a costly solution that divided the wedding guests along generational as well as musical lines. Surely one well-played clarinet could have bridged the gap between genres and generations.

One reason to start with a booking agency is that they are more likely to represent "wedding bands" who are used to playing for parties and can play everything from oldies to salsa to swing. Many couples hate the idea of a "wedding band." They have visions of Adam Sandler in *The Wedding Singer* and every bar mitzvah or Sweet 16 party they ever attended where the band leader or master of ceremonies was oily and overbearing.

However, the alternatives may not be better. A club band that has never played a wedding may play too loudly, do too few slow songs, or refuse to play "YMCA" even if the mother of the bride's sorority sisters request it. A club band doesn't always have an emcee who knows to introduce the newlyweds, their first dance, the father-daughter dance, and so on.

The bandleader will follow your lead. If the bride wants a lot of drum rolls and patter, most bandleaders are happy to oblige. If she'd prefer that the music do the talking, you can ask the emcee to shut up and play. Also, be sure to warn the leader about relatives who are likely to want to sing with the band. If, after a few drinks, Uncle Louie grabs the mike, starts snapping his fingers, and launches into his solo, the musicians will know what to do—take a break before he can get past the opening bars.

Consider the size of the room before you make a final decision. A big band in a small room can have guests running for ear cover. The banquet or facilities manager can tell you what works best in the space.

If that space is your backyard, think about your neighborhood. Assuming you aren't inviting everyone within earshot, you'll want to tune down the volume. Otherwise the late arrivals may be the police.

Even if you bond with the band, you need a contract and agreement on a playlist. The contract should cover who the musicians will be—you want to be sure that the players you hear are the ones you get. The agreement should also state how the musicians will dress, how long they'll play, how often they'll take breaks, what time they'll arrive to set up, and what their needs are for space and electrical connections.

Do you have to feed the band? Only if you want them to play well.

According to one wedding authority, 80 percent of music played at wedding receptions is provided by disc jockeys. Mostly, it's a matter of money. A deejay costs less—you're paying one person instead of a group. In addition, a deejay's equipment takes up less space, so there's more room for tables and the dance floor. A deejay's music library can be broader than a band's repertoire, and there's no question about getting top talent—instead of a wedding singer imitating Springsteen or Sinatra, you get Springsteen or Sinatra. And wedding guests never try to sing with the deejay.

Once again, you are in control. The deejay will jolly up the crowd or fade into the background—it's your call. You can submit a playlist and a "not in this lifetime" list. Meredith nixed any synchronized dances and any song "that inspires the overwhelming urge to create a conga line."

A good deejay will read the crowd and play accordingly, creating the right mix of fast and slow numbers, ethnics and oldies. Many will also create a CD for the bride, including the first dance song, the father-daughter dance song, and other memorable numbers.

The same contract rules apply to deejays and the bands. And yes, you should feed the deejay. If the deejay faints from hunger, it really puts a damper on the festivities.

Whether you hire a band or a deejay, remember that the music makers need a script as well as a score. You'll want to give the emcee or the deejay a timetable for blessings, toasts, and any ethnic dances that are "musts." If you want the bridal party to be "announced" as well as the bride and groom, tell the emcee in advance how to pronounce every name.

Despite all of your preparations and instructions, there is nothing you can do to prevent a guest from requesting the chicken dance, the macarena, the electric slide, or some other number that the bride cannot abide.

A good emcee will explain that he cannot deviate from the agreed playlist without consulting a higher authority. This is the moment when you, the mother of the bride, step in to convince the guest that what they really need is another drink, another piece of wedding cake, or an introduction to someone guaranteed to keep them far from the dance floor.

Reality Check #16

THE WEDDING SINGER

Many wedding ceremonies now include a vocal selection performed by a soloist or, in some cases, a full choir. What could be more moving than hearing the rafters ring with glorious notes of joy! However, the trend has inspired many volunteer wedding singers who have no formal training but have been told all their lives that they have lovely singing voices.

Your sister's sister-in-law's cousin may offer to sing "Ave Maria" or her own touching rendition of the Carpenters' classic "We've Only Just Begun." How can you say no?

Find a way.

This is your daughter's wedding, not *American Idol*.

Some amateur singers start strong but fade well before the final note. Others can turn a 3-minute song into an endless aria.

Even if your sister's sister-in-law's cousin is another Norah Jones or Allison Krauss, there's only room for one diva at a wedding—the bride.

17

GET THEM TO THE CHURCH ON TIME

Try explaining this to the father of the bride—counting the vehicles owned by your family, your friends, the bride, the groom, and their friends, you have a veritable fleet of cars at your disposal. But you still have to hire another one to get the bride and the wedding party to the church on time. And not just any car. It has to be a stretch limo—bridal white, not funeral black—or a classic car the likes of which you could never afford, even if you didn't have to pay for the wedding.

A trolley would be nice. A horse and carriage would also suffice. It doesn't have to be Cinderella's coach, but it does have to be shiny and fit for a princess.

Leaving the church, she'll need another romantic ride. And she has to leave the reception in style, too. Helicopter, anyone? Hot air balloon?

Like every other aspect of weddings, transportation has become more elaborate and more expensive. Nobody expects the bride to thumb a ride or crowd into the back of the family car in her wedding finery—even if the father of the bride clears out the old soft drink cups and vacuums it for the occasion. But it is still hard to explain how a luxury vehicle becomes a necessity when there's a bride inside.

Once you figure out how to transport the bride in style, you have to consider transporting the guests. Out-of-towners don't always rent cars, and some other guests may not be drivers. If the ceremony is in one place and the reception is in another, you have to think about ferrying wedding participants and wedding guests between locations.

The easiest option is to have the whole shebang in a hotel. That way you don't have to transport anybody. The bride gets dressed upstairs with the wedding party. Close family and out-of-towners will stay right there. Your transportation responsibility consists of locating the elevators and making sure that elderly or slow-moving guests start moving toward them early enough to make the ceremony.

Any venue that accommodates both the ceremony and reception will simplify transportation. Most will have dressing areas for the bridal party. The groom and his group don't have to struggle into bouffant dresses that button up the back or wrinkle easily. They can dress at home and drive themselves to the wedding.

However, if your daughter is being married in a church, a scenic garden, or some other site removed from the reception, like it or not, you have to work out the logistics for the newlyweds, the wedding party, and some or all of the guests.

First comes the bride. Transportation vendors are geared to meet her every need. They'll offer you a variety of vehicles complete with uniformed drivers, champagne on ice, music and videos, and other bridal accoutrements. Some will even roll out a red carpet for the bride and put a "just married" sign on the back for the great getaway.

The best limo drivers take their responsibilities seriously. One driver called the photographer himself when the bride's schedule changed and, once she reached the church, helped the bride with the train on her wedding dress.

If you plan to rent a limousine in May or June, you need to plan early. Brides have to compete with prom goers for limo rentals, and during prom season, some companies insist on a six- to eight-hour minimum. Major conventions can also tie up local limos. A Washington, D.C., bride discovered that the World Bank was meeting on her wedding weekend and there wasn't a limo to be had south of New York City.

When we booked a limousine for Meredith's wedding, we knew there was a three-hour minimum. We sent the limo back and forth several times to pick up the wedding party and the relatives. Even so, we paid the limo driver to cool his heels in the parking lot for hours, waiting to carry the happy couple back to the hotel after the wedding. But I'll never forget Tony's grandma and grandpa climbing into the limo with Meredith, Tony, and a bunch of bridesmaids for that ride. Priceless!

You need to be very specific when you order a limousine. There are town cars, regular limos, stretch limos, and conveyances called limousine lounges. Some companies specialize in vintage cars—from a 1933 Rolls Royce to a 1957 Bentley. (For some reason, British classic cars seem more elegant than American upstarts.) But you need to ask how many people the car can accommodate—a classic car may seat only 2 while some stretch limos can take as many as 20. You also want to check that vintage cars are in mint condition. Rusty bumpers and stained seats won't match the wedding finery.

Some "princess" brides believe that love

and marriage go together like a horse and carriage. That's doable, too. Just remind the bride that an open carriage in the rain or an unheated carriage in the freezing cold of mid-January may be a little uncomfortable. In addition, horse power is slower than engine power. According to one carriage company, a three-mile ride can take as long as 40 minutes. If you are worried about time, they suggest that you use the carriage for a block or two, long enough to impress the guests and take plenty of pictures. You can have a car meet you at an appointed spot, jump out of the carriage and into the car, and speed off to your reception.

Be sure to check references for any company you are considering and ask about the carriage drivers. Are they dressed to look like they cater to the carriage trade? Some companies will also provide a uniformed footman to help you aboard and add to the illusion of a bygone era.

Before you sign a transporation contract, read the fine print. Some companies will allow for just pickup and drop-off service. Any extra stops—to take photos, for example—may cost extra. Some begin charging you from the second the car leaves their garage. Some vendors own their own vehicles and some are only middlemen. Some include the gratuity in the price; some don't.

While you're arranging suitable transportation for the bridal couple, it is easy to forget the guests. At one wedding, the bride had arranged for a party bus to take her, the groom, and the wedding party to the reception. But many of the guests crowded on the bus first. When it was full, the bus departed, leaving several bridesmaids and groomsmen stranded in the parking lot.

We booked rooms at a hotel that offered

shuttle van service to our wedding venue. As long as we filled our block of rooms, the van service was free. The van made two trips each way to accommodate all of our out-of-town guests.

If you don't want to hire vans, trolleys, or a bus to transport the out-of-town guests to and from the wedding, you can arrange for your friends and neighbors to take outlanders along for the ride.

Guests can and do fend for themselves. Working one's way through the pews in search of a ride to the reception is one way a guest can make new friends. And if a guest doesn't make it to the reception . . . well, that's one less mouth to feed.

Will most of your guests be driving to the wedding? Then you need to think about parking. We rejected some beautiful wedding venues because they had no parking facilities and street parking nearby ranged from scarce to nonexistent.

Downtown hotels often have valet or self parking. At country clubs, historic houses, or your own house, you may have to hire a valet parking company to take care of guest cars. The going rate is around $20 to $25 per attendant, and you'll need about five valets for each 100 guests.

Or you can do what we did—find a place with a great big parking lot and no charge to use it.

WHY THE BRIDE SHOULD BE DISCOURAGED
FROM RIDING OFF TO THE RECEPTION
ON A BICYCLE, MOTORCYCLE, OR HORSE

1. She'll get her skirt stuck in the spokes.

2. Her tiara will get smashed under the motorcycle helmet.

3. She'll be splattered with mud, axle grease, or worse.

4. If they get lost, neither the groom nor the horse can be trusted to ask for directions.

Part 4

THE WEDDING POMP
AND PROTOCOL

IT'S ALL ABOUT THE DRESS

When your daughter was a little girl, she couldn't imagine what her Prince Charming would look like. But she knew what she would look like when she married him. In a word: beautiful. A beautiful girl in a beautiful dress.

Every girl deserves her fairy tale. You can't guarantee that she'll live happily ever after, but you can see that she is dressed for the part. I use the word "girl" deliberately. When it comes to her wedding, every bride is a girl no matter how old she is when she marries. And no matter how blasé she appears, she's still got that fantasy.

Take the case of the bride and groom who met as Peace Corps volunteers in Zambia. For two years she cut her hair with a Swiss Army knife. But on her wedding day, as the makeup artist applied her false eyelashes, the bride gushed, "I get to wear the Cinderella pouffy dress, so it's kind of like the end of the fairy tale."

On the surface, the Peace Corps bride would have nothing in common with an editor of a haute fashion magazine who said "I do" at age 42. But they share that little girl fantasy.

The editor had pictured herself in a

tasteful little suit or a tea-length silk party dress. Instead, encouraged by her friends, she went for what she really wanted. Her dress was pale green, but it had a skirt that billowed halfway down the block. Underneath she wore a tulle petticoat. She looked like a cross between a member of the French court and Scarlett O'Hara at Tara.

Another jaded fashionista who doubted she would ever wed saw a white silk crepe bias-cut slip dress at a John Galliano fashion show in Paris and suddenly she was a believer. When her boyfriend conveniently showed up in Paris a week later with his grandmother's Art Deco diamond ring, it was fate. She said "yes" and bought the dress.

Finding that beautiful wedding dress is like no other retail experience you and your daughter have ever had. It can be exhilarating or humiliating. It is both intensively private and incredibly public. It is at once the most and the least consumer-friendly purchase you will ever make.

Let me explain. Wedding dresses are sold in bridal boutiques or department stores with bridal salons. You can't just drop by to try on a few wedding gowns. You have to make an appointment. You will be assigned to a sales consultant who will steer you through the possibilities and go into the dressing room with your daughter to help her into each dress she tries on.

This was a shock to Meredith and me, two discount shoppers who are used to pawing through the racks unassisted and trying on garments unsupervised. Sometimes the process seemed a little too close for comfort.

You have to start looking for the dream dress about a year before the wedding. That's because wedding gowns, even gowns that are not designer originals, are custom made and can take up to six months to arrive. Then they invariably need alterations. The average bride goes for two or three fittings before the wedding.

Your daughter may have her heart set on a particular style or silhouette before she walks in the door of the first bridal salon. Even so, the two of you are likely to experience what the wedding industry calls "white blindness" when confronted with rack after rack of dresses in white, off-white, ivory, eggshell, ecru, and every shade in between. The gowns may be organized by silhouette, by style, by manufacturer, or by price—which makes it all the more confusing. Let's say your daughter thinks she wants off-white, strapless, and simple. That narrows it down to a mere 500 possibilities.

If you shop for a wedding dress on a weekend, you'll have the added confusion of a profusion of brides trying on similar dresses at the same time. Each bride arrives with her own contingent of friends, her mother, her grandmother, and sometimes her children who come to consult on the big dress decision. Most salons have several dressing rooms but only one large mirrored room where the begowned brides can see themselves and let their coterie see them in the dresses under consideration. Between the friends oohing, the mothers aahing, and the babies crying, it can be a little hard to concentrate on one girl in one gown—even if the girl is yours.

Each store has only one sample of each of the gowns it carries. It is a sample size 8 or 10—these are couture sizes that tend to be smaller than an average size 8 or 10 dress. Once your daughter decides on a dress, the salesperson will measure her bust, waist, and hips. Then the store will check the gown manufacturer's size charts and order the size that matches your daughter's biggest measurement.

Your size-10 daughter may go into shock

when the saleswoman says she'll have to order a size 14. You'll go into shock if they say she needs a size 16 or 18—you may pay a 10 to 15 percent premium for larger sizes.

The one exception is the David's Bridal chain, which stocks dresses in sizes from 2 to 26W and now accounts for 20 percent of the American bridal market. Dresses at David's are also likely to be less expensive and embellished with machine-made embroidery and lace. Does it matter how well a wedding gown is made, considering that it will only be worn once? That's between you, your daughter, and your budget.

Whoever said, "What you see is what you get," never shopped for a wedding dress. There is little correlation between appearance and price. Sometimes you are paying for hand-beading or lace. We couldn't tell the difference. Sometimes you are paying for the label. Say "Vera Wang," "Carolina Herrera," or "Badgely Mischka," and

the price goes up. If the dress is a one-of-a-kind designer original, the price goes waaaay up.

Couture designers have traditionally ended their fashion shows with a bride in a wedding dress—but, off the runway, most of them never produced wedding dresses. Now that the couture market has shriveled and the wedding market has boomed, more name designers are eager to dress brides.

Vera Wang is a different story. She started out in the 1980s as a bridal retailer and became a designer when she couldn't find gowns she liked in the bridal market. Wang does use fabulous fabrics, and her gowns fit and flatter svelte figures. Uma Thurman, Sharon Stone, and Mariah Carey were wed in Wang. (Disclaimer: The demise of their subsequent marriages cannot be blamed on their wedding gowns!)

Wang has had a profound influence on

the wedding industry—simpler, graceful gowns are now available at every price level. Vera Wang has also become a wedding conglomerate, marketing everything from gowns to accessories to perfume to china.

According to www.brides.com, 83 percent of brides want to lose weight before their wedding days. There is a temptation to order the dress in a smaller size as an incentive. If the bridal salon goes along with this cockamamie idea, run—do not walk—to the nearest exit. (In some salons, if the bride insists, the salon will order a smaller size but the bride has to authorize the purchase in writing.)

Taking in a dress is relatively easy—coming up with extra fabric and matching beading or embroidery to let a dress out is not. I watched a bride in tears during her final fitting when it was clear that her dress would not zip. The wedding was two weeks away. I hoped that she would be able to weep nonstop for a fortnight to lose enough water weight so the dress would close. If not, she was going to need a really big shawl.

Alterations can make or break a wedding gown. "The dream dress turned out to be a nightmare," one mother of the bride told me. Her daughter picked a simple dress with a huge train. After the first fitting, the dress was buckling at the seams. By the second fitting, the bride had lost weight. The shop's fitters were not very accommodating. By the time she left the shop, the bride was crying hysterically. She was afraid that the dress would either gape or pull too tightly on her wedding day.

Both mother and bride were so upset that nobody focused on instructions for bustling the long train after the ceremony.

Halfway through the reception, the bustle started listing badly. Fortunately, the videographer, no stranger to bridal bustles, was able to get the train under control.

You may think that bustles went out with whalebone stays. They are still a staple of wedding wear. The bride's train becomes a bustle through a complicated arrangement of fabric and hooks or buttons. In theory, the bustle keeps the bride from tripping. In practice, it often keeps the guests from dinner while the bride and her handmaidens try to remember which fabric attaches to which hook. If your daughter's dress has a train, make sure there is more than one friend who knows how the bustle works.

The process of buying a wedding gown is so complex that it is as important to shop for a bridal shop as it is to shop for the dress itself. You are relying on the shop to help you select the right dress, order it in the right size, alter it to fit perfectly, and stay in business long enough to do all of the above. In addition, once you buy the wedding dress, a bridal shop will often discount additional purchases you make there, including the veil, the headpiece, the shoes, and the bridesmaids' dresses.

Meanwhile, back in the dressing room, your daughter will be trying on a lot of dresses that don't fit and trying to reconcile her mental ideal with the image in the mirror. If your daughter is smaller than the sample, the salesperson will pull the dress back with giant clothespins to give her an idea of how it will look. If your daughter is larger than the sample, she'll hold it up unzipped and try to imagine the full effect.

It helps if the bride is wearing the right underwear—a strapless bra accommodates almost all styles. She can bring her own shoes, but most salons have shoes in several heel heights to help you both visualize the final effect.

You are a huge part of the dress-buying process—so much so that the wedding industry refers to the instant that a bride looks at herself in the mirror and realizes that she has found her dream dress as the "Oh, Mommy Moment." It ought to be the opportunity for incredible closeness, but it often turns out to be the moment of greatest conflict.

That's because brides and mothers often have very different ideas about what's appropriate for the walk down the aisle. Many mothers were married in an era when modesty was a major requirement.

"You hear the mothers saying, doesn't she need sleeves, shouldn't her shoulders be covered?" reports a longtime bridal consultant. The mothers are thinking "the Madonna," and the daughters are thinking just "Madonna."

The difference in perception about proper bridal attire can ruin a wedding for both mother and daughter. A Virginia bride was pleased when her mother offered to pay for her wedding dress, even though the couple were paying for their own wedding. The bride found a strapless gown on sale at Macy's and breathlessly called her mother to come to see it. When she described the dress, her mother was horrified.

"What will your aunts say? What will the priest say?" the mother asked coldly.

They argued over the phone for a solid hour. The bride left Macy's in tears. She ended up waiting until four weeks before the wedding to buy a dress off the rack at David's. On her wedding day, she got dressed at a friend's house, not at her mother's.

A year later, the rift has not healed.

"The irony is that she's a family counselor at the church," the bride said bitterly.

Other mothers equate weddings with lace, beading, and other embellishments. One mother nixed her daughter's choice because the dress was so simple she thought it looked like a nightgown.

Seventy percent of the dresses sold today are strapless, reports Mara Urshel. She ought to know. Urshel is the owner of Kleinfeld, a Brooklyn bridal salon that draws 12,000 brides a year from all over the world. Founded in 1941, the store now takes up half a city block in Bay Ridge, not a neighborhood normally associated with high fashion.

And still they come. Designer Isaac Mizrahi, a Brooklyn boy, says, "If you can't find it at Kleinfeld, you should cancel the wedding." The day I was there, a bride from Cairo (Egypt, not Illinois) was in for her final fitting.

At any given moment, Kleinfeld has 1,000 sample dresses ranging from over-the-top fantasy styles to understated elegance and costing from $1,200 to "If you have to ask, you can't afford it." The fantasy dresses are just that—their huge skirts and flounces evoke every Cinderella vision you or your daughter ever had. Compared to some of these dresses, Princess Di was married in a bedsheet!

One room is devoted to Orthodox Jewish or conservative Christian brides who still seek to keep themselves covered. At the other extreme are dresses for women who work hard to stay in shape and want the world to know it. Some of these are by Elie Saab—body-conscious gowns like the one he designed for actress Halle Berry when she won the Academy Award.

There are also dresses designed especially for destination weddings—simple, light, and easily transportable. There are dresses for drama queens and dresses for self-proclaimed simple souls.

(This last group is not always the easiest to please. A lot of brides say they are looking for a very simple strapless dress with no beads, ruffles, embroidery, or lace. But they want their dress to be "unique." While they are searching for this impossible dress, their mothers are tearing their hair out.)

Every weekend Kleinfeld holds trunk shows with more new dresses. With so many choices, it is no wonder brides tend to get confused. Urshel likens the bridal sales consultant to a wine steward at a fine restaurant. They can make educated recommendations, leading you to dresses you or your daughter might not even have considered.

That is what happened to us.

Meredith had a stack of pictures and a clear idea of what she wanted—tight bodice, big skirt, not strapless, and no beads or baubles. We saw some nice dresses at the first bridal salon we visited. But we were there on a weekend—a big mistake.

Next we tried one of the tonier salons in town—the kind of place that outfits ladies for inaugural balls and state occasions. There weren't many wedding dresses on display, but our saleswoman assured us that she had the perfect dress. "It looks good on everybody," she said.

It was strapless, with a sash and a wide skirt. It looked good on Meredith, but it was pricey. And we were uneasy about a dress that looked good on everybody. Was this a subtle insult: "It looks good on everybody, even a lump like you?" Would we see armies of brides marching down aisles in this very dress?

Our third stop proved to be the best bet. It was in a dreary strip mall in Manassas, Virginia, and had an unimposing name— Jeanette's Bride 'N' Tux Boutique. Jeanette's had acres of dresses and a cheery Brit named Joan Brightman to lead us through them. Within an hour, Meredith found her dress.

It wasn't what she thought she wanted. The bodice was embroidered with silvery beads, and matching beadwork circled the hem. Several dresses she expected to love overwhelmed my 5-foot, 2-inch daughter.

When she came out of the dressing room, she looked regal. It was our "Oh, Mommy Moment." But I didn't tear up until Joan added a veil. Suddenly she wasn't a girl in a prom dress—she was a bride.

In the months between buying the dress and wearing it, most brides have one overriding concern—will I look fat? Women often grow up with the notion that they must be in perfect shape on their wedding day. Without their faithful ally, basic black,

they panic. "It's the fear of the 'waving waddle,'" says Sue Fleming, the personal trainer behind the Buff Brides phenomenon. No matter how good they look to the groom, they think they need to look better.

The popularity of strapless, backless dresses only increases the pressure on brides-to-be. Not only are the dresses more revealing, but also every ounce of extra flesh is captured in living color by the ever-present photographer and videographer. It is enough to turn many women into quivering masses of protoplasm or send them into cardio and cabbage soup frenzy. The condition is common enough to have a name—bridalexia.

If weight has ever been an issue for your daughter, it is likely to surface now. If it has been an issue between the two of you, she may be dreading the day you mention "diet."

My mother was a dedicated weight

watcher—only the weight that she watched was mine. Throughout my life, shopping expeditions were a race to see whether she would get disgusted first or I would get hives first. I dreaded shopping with her for a wedding gown.

But the patron saint of brides, Our Lady of Perpetual List Making, was watching over me. For the first and only time in my life, stress made me lose my appetite. (It is a condition I have tried and failed to replicate ever since.) By the time I tried on my first wedding dress, I was just thin enough to please my mother.

It is hard for a bride to feel beautiful if her mother treats her like a work in progress. This is the time to remind her—and remember yourself—that beautiful brides come in a variety of sizes and shapes. The plus-size bride has a lot of lovely dresses to choose from now—not a white muumuu among them.

Price was a major issue in our house. That is because my husband, Benjamin, has a friend in New Delhi who knew of a factory in India that could copy any dress Meredith wanted for $400. In fact, Benjamin was so taken with the idea that he talked about setting up a company to sell Indian-made wedding dresses on the Internet. Meredith and I were less enchanted with the idea of sending off a photo and getting back a dress sight unseen. We declined the offer, but we did stay out of the stratosphere when we went dress shopping.

If your daughter is not fixated on the idea of the one-and-only dream dress, or she is open to cost-effective alternatives, there are ways to save on a wedding dress:

Borrow a dress from a friend or relative. Of course, it helps if both brides are the same size and body type. You'll have to return it dry-cleaned, in pristine condition, but that cost is negligible compared to the purchase price.

Recycle a family heirloom. "I once had a family of five daughters wear the same dress," Mara Urshel reports. "With alterations it fit all of them." But you have to be willing to allow the dress to be restyled, if necessary. If it requires a total overhaul, it may not be much less expensive than buying a new dress. But if wearing a mother's or grandmother's dress has sentimental value, it is worth the price.

Buy a previously worn dress. A designer dress you could never afford new may be available at the right price on eBay or a local consignment shop.

Plan to resell the dress right after the wedding. One New York bride bought a $6,000 dress with the express intention of selling it on eBay right after the wedding for $2,500. When questioned about her lack of romantic attachment to the gown, she replied, "What am I going to do? Put it on and walk through Central Park?"

Get a great bargain. Since 1947, Filene's, the famed Boston retailer, has been famous for the annual bridal gown sale where more than 1,000 gowns ranging in price from $850 to $3,000 are sold for less than $250 each. (There are a few high-end designer dresses in the mix that go for $499.) In 2003, Filene's held their first wedding gown sales in Atlanta, Washington, and New York as well as Boston. Brides and their families line up the night before to be among the first through the door, grab as many dresses as they can, and try them on amid the crowds of other brides and families. This is a team effort. Brides need help grabbing dresses, trading the ones they don't want with other bridal parties, and staking out a spot on the selling floor near a mirror for use as a dressing room. Most brides are prepared to strip in public—they wear sports bras and shorts.

It takes gumption, endurance, and imagination to score at the Filene's sale—many dresses will need lots of alterations to work. But I saw more than a few Carolina Herreras go out the door for a pittance compared to their regular price.

Reality Check #18

WHY YOUR DAUGHTER DOESN'T WANT TO WEAR YOUR WEDDING DRESS

1. It's a size 2 and she's a size 10.

2. It's the right size but it isn't her style.

3. You were married in a meadow, and she's getting married in a cathedral.

4. She thinks it makes her look fat.

5. She thinks it makes her look just like you.

19

AND THE BRIDE'S MOTHER WORE . . .

Pick up a bridal magazine or enter a bridal salon and you are instantly aware that brides have come a long way, baby. Gone are the days when the bride was expected to be modestly attired. Today she can wear what she likes—corset tops, kimono sleeves, mermaid tails, or slit skirts. Top fashion designers vie to catch her eye. She can also dress her bridesmaids in a host of styles that wouldn't be out of place at a sexy soiree.

But nobody wants to dress the mother of the bride.

Every bridal salon has a dark corner reserved for mother-of-the-bride dresses. They hang forlornly, ashamed of their outdated sequined, jacketed styles. Most of them would be equally appropriate for the grandmother of the bride or the great-grandmother of the bride. Mothers of brides may be younger, fitter, and hipper than ever before, but you'd never know it from the dresses deemed suitable for Mama.

The wedding cake is better dressed than the mother of the bride!

We shouldn't take this personally. Even mothers known for their beauty and style are ignored at their children's weddings. Does anybody remember what Jackie

Kennedy Onassis wore to her daughter Caroline's wedding? What Queen Elizabeth wore when Prince Charles married Diana? When Vera Wang's daughter gets married, will anybody notice that Vera Wang is wearing a Vera Wang?

Media accounts of weddings treat most brides as if they were motherless children.

There are pictures of the fathers, the children, the bridesmaids, the groomsmen, the pets, the ministers, the florists, the caterers, the musicians, and the guests. But rarely is there a mother in sight.

As a result, mothers of brides often go to extremes. There are the Red Hot Mamas, slinking down the aisle in form-fitting strapless dresses that scream "I've still got it, honey." And there are the Lavender and Lace Mamas, wearing what is expected of them and fading into the background.

Of course, I was determined not to be either one. The Red Hot Mama option was out. I wish I could say that I rejected it on principle. The truth is that I would have looked like a bratwurst in a tight, strapless dress. But the idea of looking like my own grandmother wasn't appealing either.

When Meredith got engaged, I wasn't exactly in great shape. But I promised myself that by the time of the wedding, I would be a mere shadow of my former self. I would not need to hide any unfortunate flab under a jacket, a stole, or layers of floaty chiffon.

Meredith was getting married on a Saturday night in June. She and I agreed that a long dress would be appropriate. I managed to stall dress shopping until January. By that time I realized that:

Formal gowns, like wedding dresses, have to be ordered months in advance.

Most stores do not stock a wide range of sizes and colors, so the dress you try probably won't fit and won't be in the color you want.

Short of scheduling a few sessions on the rack, I wasn't going to get tall enough or thin enough to look good in most formal dresses.

Never tell a salesperson that you are looking for a mother-of-the-bride dress. If you do, they'll steer you right to the jacket-dress-with-sequins section.

My first forays into the posh salons that sell "special occasion" dresses were not pretty. I tried on a beige chiffon number that pooled around my feet and made me look like a butterscotch sundae. I tried on a lavender prom dress with a tight waist and a full skirt—a silhouette that didn't flatter me when I was young enough to wear it. I tried on dresses cut so low in the back and the front that they barely covered my embarrassment.

After several discouraging shopping trips,

I told the mother of the groom not to wait for me to buy my dress first. Meredith did not care what color we each wore. There was little likelihood that we would end up with the same dress since the groom's mother is a petite redhead and I'm a buxom bottle blond.

As January morphed into February and then March marched on, I began to panic. I finally found a dress where I least expected to—in my daughter's bridal salon. The owner had to talk me into trying it. It had very little "hanger appeal." In addition, I was wearing black trouser socks and bad underwear at the time. But the dress was flattering—or it would be with the right shoes and a little help from the proper undergarments. It was a two-piece knit dress with short, scalloped sleeves, a scooped neck, and a scalloped hem. It was also lavender and lace. The bride loved it. I . . . liked it very much.

I ended up looking exactly like what I was—the mother of the bride.

Talking to other mothers, I've discovered that there are a lot of creative ways to look your best, look like yourself, and still please the bride.

Forget the rules about what is "appropriate" for morning or evening, indoors or outside. The only rule that counts is that the bride makes the rules. You can't outshine or embarrass her. If she wants a long white dress and a cathedral veil to walk through the woods for her sylvan ceremony, she should have it. If you and she agree that you'll wear a pantsuit and pearls to the ceremony, that's fine too. Lightning will not strike if you are less formal than the bride or others in the wedding party.

Ignore the fashionistas. Look for a dress that looks good on you, even if it isn't the waistline, hemline, or sleeve line that is "in" this season. Bridal gowns don't change much from season to season, so there is no reason that the mother of the bride should be bound by the vagaries of fashion. As long as your outfit doesn't have linebacker shoulder pads, a bare midriff, or enough bugle beads to play taps, it will be stylish enough for the occasion.

Think twice about any dress that requires a shawl and a stole. You'll fiddle with it, have your hands full with it, and probably land one end in the soup.

Shop where you normally do. You don't need to go to a specialty store. Most department stores stock party clothes that don't fit the mother-of-the-bride stereotypes.

Shop vintage. Look for vintage stores where the ladies who lunch and attend charity balls recycle their clothes. You may find couture bargains and styles from more forgiving eras.

Look at bridesmaid's dresses. These dresses often have simple, flattering lines and come in lots of colors. Just be sure you don't pick the same dress or dress fabric as the actual bridesmaids.

Have a dress made. Pick a dress you've always felt beautiful wearing and have it copied in a color and fabric that works for the wedding.

Have a dress remade. The mother of the groom found a strapless dress she liked, but she didn't like herself in a strapless dress. She had sleeves made from the matching stole that came with the dress.

Find a few easy pieces. One mother of the bride wore a ball skirt and a beautiful organdy blouse to her daughter's wedding. Another wore a satin tunic and pants ensemble.

It's not just the dress that counts—it's what's under the dress. And I'm not talking about your heart of gold. I'm talking about Lycra, industrial strength Lycra, the mother of the bride's best friend. The kind of Lycra that deserves an Oscar for best supporting role. Lycra can hold it in, push it up, and smooth it out. No mother of the bride should go out without it.

In every city, there is at least one store that specializes in Lycra. Invariably, it has tiny little lacy underthings in the window. But step inside and you'll find the kind of undergarments that mean business.

As soon as I bought my mother-of-the-bride dress, I headed to my local Lycra emporium. I went into the dressing room with two garments designed to smooth me from neck to knee. Some of these garments should come with warning labels. They require a considerable amount of strength and dexterity to pull up or down and into place.

At one point, I had a "body suit" around my waist like a tourniquet. I felt myself getting faint. I started to sweat. But I refused to call for help from the size-2 sales assistant who stood outside the dressing room. I did get the thing on and, aside from the fact that I couldn't breathe, it was an amazing transformation.

I did not buy the miracle garment. Instead I chose a lighter-weight body suit, a less painful alternative. Now that I have seen the wedding pictures, I realize that I made a big mistake. Sure, I would have breathed less in the body armor, but I would have bulged less, too.

Comfort is rarely the primary consideration in wedding attire. Wedding shoes are rarely made for walking, let alone dancing. It is a wise mother who has two pairs of wedding shoes—one pair for walking down the aisle and taking pictures, a second pair to wear during the party afterward. If you're wearing a long dress, you'll need to find two pairs with about the same heel height—or be prepared to hike up your skirt once you put on your comfortable shoes.

If the wedding is outside, on grass or gravel, try walking on that surface before you buy your shoes. Skinny heels sink into grass and gravel.

You'll also want to wear your wedding shoes before the wedding, even if it's only around the house. If you're worried about slipping on stairs or marble floors, you can try the models' runway trick—they put masking tape on the soles of shoes to give them traction. Or scuff the souls with an emery board.

Formal wedding shoes are downright utilitarian compared to the tiny purses that go with party clothes. Most barely accommodate a hankie and two breath mints.

That's fine as long as you can stash a tote with the stuff you really need somewhere on the premises. If the ceremony and the reception are in two different locations, ask a friend to make sure your tote gets to the party.

Weddings do afford one privilege to the mother of the bride—this is your chance to bring out the bling. Most of us have jewelry that stays locked away because our casual lifestyles offer no opportunities to wear it. This is your chance to get out the emerald necklace or diamond brooch you inherited from your mother or grandmother and wear it with pride. You are old enough to carry it off now, and wouldn't your mother or grandmother be proud to see you shine.

No precious metal in the family coffers? Then behave like the star you are and borrow some. I had a jewelry crisis at Meredith's wedding. Benjamin had taken the family heirloom bracelet out of the vault the day before the wedding, but I never tried it on. When we got to the wedding, no one could open the clasp.

I am proud to say that I did not panic. I simply went to cousin Gloria, the Baroness of Bling, and borrowed two of the bracelets she was wearing.

My daughter was engaged for 16 months—plenty of time to consider any number of treatments to make me look younger and prettier and . . . younger. The idea of looking at my unadulterated self in countless wedding pictures and on the wedding video made me blanch.

There are three reasons that a woman gets a face-lift, according to a noted Los Angeles plastic surgeon:

    She is starting to look like her mother.

She's going to a class reunion.

Her daughter is getting married.

"But I don't want to upstage the bride," I told my husband. He laughed undiplomatically. Clearly, there was no chance of that.

I opted not to have cosmetic surgery. It wasn't due to any commitment to growing old gracefully. It was naked fear. I'm not the world's quickest healer. Even my skin bears grudges. I was afraid that I might not recover fast enough to look good in the wedding pictures.

There is always a chance that even minor procedures can backfire. A friend was convinced to have her eyebrows waxed two weeks before her daughter's wedding. She had an allergic reaction to the wax and emerged with two angry red rectangles framing her eyebrows. "It calmed down by the wedding day, but not a lot," she recalls.

If you're planning major changes in your face, your hair color, or your hairstyle, try them well before the wedding. Even with "lunch-hour makeovers" like botox or dermabrasion, you may look worse before you look better.

What about those facial exercise gadgets that promise a nonsurgical face-lift? A well-respected dermatologist told me that they do work. But it can take months before you see a difference and, as with so many other things, I didn't start early enough.

So I worked out with a trainer, tried to watch my diet, and bought heels high enough to make me look a little taller. I also tried something that promised an instant, if temporary, face-lift. It's called Years Away Beauty Lifts. You glue one end of a thin elastic band behind your ear, stretch it under your hair to the other ear, and glue the other end down. This effectively pulls your skin back. If your hair is long enough, you can do another band in the neck area.

Supposedly, celebrities use these things all the time. Maybe they have better glue. In practice, my bands kept popping. I felt like I was back in junior high, wearing braces with rubber bands that had a life of their own. Sure, I wanted to feel young, but not that young.

A month before the wedding, I decided that I'd look better in lavender with a tan, so I went to one of those sunless tanning places. The first time, my feet turned orange and I missed a few spots. The second time, the week of the wedding, I asked to have the machine adjusted a little, and I "baked" to a nice tan color.

A good makeup artist also worked minor miracles. There's nothing like a little paint and false eyelashes to make an old girl look like she's got new tricks.

Reality Check #19

HOW TO TELL THAT YOUR PREWEDDING PRIMPING WORKED

Nobody oohs and aahs when the mother of the bride walks down the aisle. Here's the most you can hope for:

1. I hear she's been on "South Beach."
2. She must have found a new hairdresser.
3. Botox!
4. Lipo and botox!
5. Did she do just her eyes or the whole face?

20

ANNIE, GET YOUR GLUE GUN

As the mother of the bride, I expected to "make" the wedding. But I never dreamed I would actually have to make the wedding. As soon as my daughter got engaged, my entire family came down with Martha Stewart syndrome. The primary symptom— an insane desire to grow, build, design, decorate, arrange, glue, staple, sand, or bake everything so we could "personalize" the wedding.

At first, I did not understand what they were talking about. Tony and Meredith were pledging their bodies and souls to each other. How much more personal can you get?

I had a lot to learn.

Benjamin went online and discovered we could buy flowers wholesale and arrange them ourselves. Meredith came up with the idea of growing butterflies that we could release on her wedding day. She talked about growing potted plants as favors. And she also went online to find new and exciting do-it-yourself projects for all of us.

How about getting friends and family to decorate squares that could be sewn together to form a quilt for her wedding canopy?

Sewn? Sewn by whom? Surely she wasn't

thinking of her mother, the woman whose last major sewing project was a circle skirt in eighth grade home economics. Of course she was—because it looked so easy in the creative wedding book.

It is easy to say that if you didn't have strange compulsions that involved floral clay and baling wire, you wouldn't be reading creative crafts books in the first place. But virtually every wedding resource encourages brides to be creative. And every mother who stayed up past midnight to finish a Girl Scout project so her daughter could earn a merit badge in decoupage knows what that means—more work for mother.

Why should you buy placecards, table numbers, and programs when you can make your own paper and learn calligraphy to letter them yourself? Why purchase ordinary favors when you can make your own candles, bags of sachet, or picture frames?

You too can make lanterns for your daughter's garden wedding, according to a book called *The Perfect Wedding Details*. All you need are wooden dowels and sheets of cellophane from a photo supply store. The author's mother spent the summer before her wedding making 100 of them. She suggests that the bride invite her girlfriends to a prewedding party to make favors or decorations—filling little muffin papers with fennel, dried lavender, or feathers to throw at the bridal couple, perhaps. Or baking individual fruit pies to send home with the guests as sweet favors.

These projects always look easy until you start reading the directions in small print. For example, the escort cards that tell guests where they are seated at the reception are usually just put out on a table in alphabetical order. How boring! Instead, *Martha Stewart Weddings* explains that you can get a boxwood wreath and add paper leaves printed with the guests names and table numbers:

"Using our template (see the guide), trace leaf shapes onto sturdy colored paper, then cut out. Trim edges with decorative paper edgers. Glue 22-gauge cloth-wrapped floral wire to the back of each leaf, and insert into 14-inch-diameter boxwood wreath, in alphabetical order. A 14-inch wreath will hold about 60 cards. Use multiple wreaths or a larger one for more guests. Hang with ribbon."

Right. I always have 22-gauge cloth-wrapped floral wire around the house. It is right next to my calligraphy pen and my pastry brush!

The pressure to personalize is enhanced by all of those Handy Andreas who relish the idea of baking the wedding cake or sewing heirloom lace on the bridal veil. If your daughter is one of them, by all means encourage her to craft her heart out. Just remind her of everything else she has to do before the wedding. Does she really have time to create 20 tabletop topiaries ("Cover a small portion of a polystyrene ball with hot glue, then stick rosebuds onto the ball one at a time until the entire ball is covered . . .") for the table centerpieces a week before the wedding?

If you are the crafty one, make sure your daughter wants you to demonstrate your deftness with pastry or pottery before you make plans or buy supplies.

Meredith did get her patchwork canopy, but it wasn't sewn by me. My clever friend Judy Goldman put it together as her wedding present and she loved doing it. If you or the bride have friends or relatives known for their crafts or culinary skills, enlist them to help. Be sure to tell them that their efforts are the best present they could give the happy couple. Nobody expects them to come with a chafing dish, too!

We personalized Meredith's wedding only in ways that would not require any effort on the wedding weekend. Since Tony works for a bottled water company, he had special labels printed with a picture of the two of them and the legend "Meredith and Tony, June 21, 2003. Thank you for sharing our special day."

Meredith teaches children with severe disabilities. Instead of favors, we made a contribution to a fund to build an accessible playground at her school. The gift was explained in the wedding program.

Instead of butterflies, we released Meredith and Tony.

(A few months later, I read a report about a wedding where guests were given little boxes with butterflies to release. Unfortunately, some of the butterflies died in confinement. As one of the guests remarked, "Nothing says 'I love you' like a dead butterfly.")

Before you pick up a glue gun, here are some things to think about:

Know thyself and thy family. If you are all thumbs, you won't suddenly develop woodworking skills.

Do not assume that you will save money. Of course, Meredith's chuppah quilt is priceless. But for what we paid for the fabric, the ribbon to connect the squares, the masking tape, the cutting guides, the fabric markers, the envelopes, the postage to send the squares out and get them back, and the replacement squares, pens, and envelopes for those who messed up the first time they tried to create a masterpiece, we probably could have bought a canopy by Gucci.

Do not assume everybody will share your enthusiasm. Bridesmaids didn't sign on to make centerpieces. Siblings aren't eager to spray-paint candelabras. Wedding guests don't want to work for their supper.

We discovered that while some friends and relatives loved the idea of contributing to Meredith's chuppah quilt, others felt total panic at the prospect of their "art" being on display.

⌒ Don't expect professional results. Buying the calligraphy pen doesn't make you a calligrapher. Only you can decide how much time and talent you have to master the skills you need to address invitations with professional flourish or bake a wedding cake that doesn't topple over.

⌒ Beware of projects that have to be done on the wedding weekend. Do you want to spend the hours before the wedding beautifying the hall or beautifying yourself?

⌒ There are lots of ways to "get personal" without personal exposure to hardware and hot glue. Let the couple create a signature drink to be served at the reception—you'll save on the bar bill, too! They can express themselves through the wedding vows, food, the flowers, the music, and the wedding decor.

One couple had life-size ice sculptures of their dogs atop their buffet table. A couple who met at Club Med had the resort's famous white-chocolate bread flown in for the reception. A pair of fast-food lovers arranged to have white-gloved waiters with silver trays serve Egg McMuffins and fries in the wee hours at the end of their reception. When a bride named Robyn married a groom named Jay, they commissioned a glass blower to create a robin and a blue jay to put on top of their wedding cake. They didn't have to worry about the glass birds dying or dive-bombing the guests.

Reality Check #20

PROJECTS EVEN DO-IT-YOURSELF MOTHERS SHOULDN'T DO

1. Hiring your son's Boy Scout troop to pitch the party tent

2. Anything involving a glass cutter, a blow-torch, or a chain saw

3. Creating a wedding cake with Twinkies and Reddi-wip

4. Anything you have to replicate 20 times

5. Anything that needs to be fed and watered

6. Growing your own grapes and pressing them into wine

7. Getting ordained so that you can be both minister and mother of the bride

21

WHEN DOES THE BAGPIPER JUMP THE BROOM?

There is nothing like a wedding to bring back memories of the old country—even if you never lived there yourself. Rites of passage often inspire a desire to reclaim your roots. There is no doubt that ethnic traditions add richness and depth to a wedding. They can also be a source of tension between the generations.

Your daughter may welcome the chance to embrace the old ways in her wedding. Or she may resent the imposition of rituals that have no meaning for her and her groom. Regardless of the strength of your convictions, you cannot require her to feel the same way that you do about your traditions.

Some parents who never actively practiced the religion of their ancestors are still hurt when their children don't want to be married in the church, synagogue, or temple. It is unfair to expect your daughter to "get religion" in time for the wedding. She may agree out of respect for your wishes, but if she is strongly opposed to the idea of a traditional wedding, she shouldn't be strong-armed into it.

On the other hand, sometimes the pressure to revive traditions comes from a fiancé who becomes so enamored of the other's culture that he or she seems to be joining the other side. One Sikh woman planned to have a nondenominational ceremony with one Sikh blessing. Her Christian groom fell in love with the idea of wearing a turban. As a result, the couple had two weddings: one Sikh and one nondenominational.

The groom's family feared that he was abandoning his Christian heritage. Not so. After the wedding weekend, the groom took off his turban and the couple returned to their secular lifestyle.

The moral of the story: One wedding ritual does not signify a lifelong conversion.

Sometimes it is the parents who are surprised by a young couple's desire to revive rites of the past. Many African-American couples now jump the broom. During slave days, African-Americans could not legally marry. Jumping the broom was a formal and public declaration of a couple's commitment to each other. Since some of the brides may never have seen a broom, let alone wielded one, the mother of the bride may be called upon to supply the ceremonial broom and to explain that jumping the DustBuster will not have the same effect.

It is important to recognize that you are treading on sacred, sensitive ground when you talk about traditions. If the bride and groom share a single ethnic tradition and the same degree of affection for that tradition, this may not be an issue. If the two are walking melting pots, it isn't so easy. The bride alone can have four grandparents with four different religions and national origins. And each grandparent had four grandparents with their own old-country traditions. Pick one heritage and you antagonize all of the others.

National origin sometimes counts for

more than religion when it comes to wedding traditions. An Irish wedding is nothing like an Italian wedding or a Polish wedding, although all three may take place in the same Catholic church. A northern Italian wedding may be nothing like a southern Italian wedding. In the old country, when a Sicilian wed a Milanese, it was considered a mixed marriage. It is still that way in Washington, except that here a mixed marriage is between a liberal and a conservative.

How can you sort through all of the ethnic allegiances?

It helps to recognize how much of what we think of as all-American wedding traditions were really stolen from somewhere else. According to *Bride's* magazine, the first bridal shower took place in Holland. A Dutch girl fell in love with a poor miller, and her father considered him such a poor prospect that he refused to hand over her dowry. Sympathetic friends showered the lovers with gifts so they could start their life together. It was the first dutch treat.

Romance has very little to do with enduring wedding customs. Most of the rituals we practice faithfully are all about promoting fertility and avoiding evil spirits.

Bridal bouquets started out as bunches of herbs carried by Roman brides to symbolize fertility. The Romans left nothing to chance. In case the herbs weren't enough, they broke a thin loaf of bread over the bride's head.

Wheat was another symbol of fertility. This may have been the precursor of the modern wedding cake and the tradition of smashing it into the faces of the bridal couple.

Why do brides toss their bouquets? Originally, the toss was an act of self-preservation. Wedding guests used to tear at the bride's clothes and her bouquet to grab a piece of her good luck. It can still get ugly. At some weddings, single women have elbowed each other out of the way of the bouquet. One eager bridesmaid was so enthusiastic in her pursuit of the bouquet that she leapt upward with such force that she parted company with the top of her strapless gown. Her near-Olympic high jump was captured for immortality and can be viewed on the Internet. Some brides are skipping this ritual altogether to avoid the impression that their unmarried friends are desperately seeking husbands.

The tradition of tossing the bride's garter had similarly ignominious origins. In the Middle Ages, wedding guests invaded the bridal chamber to steal the bride's stockings—another way to share her good fortune. The groom tossed out a garter to forestall the crowd. In another variation on the theme, Elizabethan-era English maidens stalked the couple to the bridal suite and tried to steal the groom's stocking. Whoever succeeded in throwing it backward over her head from the foot of the bed, hitting the groom, was promised that she would be married within the year.

Evil spirits figure in several wedding traditions. Bridesmaids and ushers were originally dressed like the bride and groom so that onlookers with evil intentions wouldn't be able to pick out the happy couple in the crowd.

The tradition of carrying the bride over the threshold is another Roman relic. Since evil spirits hovered over the threshold, the groom had to carry the bride into their new house. (Like many couples, Meredith and Tony lived together before they married. But she did insist that he carry her over the threshold of their hotel room after the wedding.)

And now for something blue. Brides in ancient Israel wore a blue ribbon on the border of their fringed robes to symbolize modesty, fidelity, and love. Early Christians wore blue because it symbolized the purity of the Virgin Mary.

In fact, white as the bridal color of choice is a fairly recent invention. In many parts of the world, brides wear red. White is reserved for mourning. White also symbolized affluence. Only a wealthy bride could afford a dress that dirtied so easily that it could only be worn once.

The wedding ring didn't start out as a token of love and fidelity. Originally, it was a considered a partial payment for the bride. These days, the engagement ring is viewed as the down payment on eternal bliss. Romantic grooms often purchase the ring without the bride, the better to present it on bended knee. (It is unseemly for the would-be bride to pull out a jeweler's loupe and assess the stone on the spot. She should wait until she gets home.)

Linking love and money is best done delicately at a wedding. The dollar or money dance is a traditional part of Latino and some other ethnic weddings. Guests throw coins at the newlyweds' feet, fill the couple's shoes with money, pin bills to the couple's clothing, or pay for the privilege of dancing with the bride or groom. But if it is not part of your cultural tradition, the dollar dance smacks of unbridled greed—almost like selling tickets to the wedding. Besides, a wad of ones can make a big show at the wedding and a very small wedding gift afterward.

The traditions of throwing rice and tying old shoes to the getaway car also have ancient roots. Rice was the symbol of plenty—and of course, fertility—in Asian cultures. In China, a red slipper was thrown onto the roof of the house as an ancient "Do Not Disturb" sign to show that the honeymoon was in progress. The Anglo-Saxon groom hit his bride on the head with a shoe to show who was the boss. Today's metrosexual groom wouldn't dream of destroying his Bruno Maglis. He also risks counterattack by his weight-lifting wife wielding a stiletto—heel, that is.

The old Teutons started the tradition of the "honeymoon." Since kidnapping was the only courtship in Teuton circles, the groom often kept the bride under wraps so that her family could not find her until she was in the family way, so to speak. The groomsmen had a special role—they helped the groom fend off the bride's family.

Once they were wed, the newlyweds imbibed a fermented honey drink called mead for the first 30 days after the wedding, or until the moon waned. By the time they sobered up, the bride was either too pregnant or too hungover to protest the marriage.

Since we have already borrowed so many wedding traditions and chosen to ignore their original intentions, brides today can feel free about borrowing a few more or marrying several strains. However, there are some traditions so tied to a group that they cannot be adapted to others. Jumping the broom is a ritual usually reserved for African-Americans. Breaking a glass at the end of the marriage ceremony is only appropriate when either the bride or the groom is Jewish. Both of these rites evoke periods of great sadness in their people's history. While there are many modern interpretations for the groom's symbolic breaking of the glass at a Jewish wedding, the traditional explanation is that the glass represents the destruction of the temple in Jerusalem. It is a classic example of Jewish guilt: "Who said you had the right to be so happy?"

That said, you should also welcome spontaneous acts of ecumenism. At one wedding, the band segued from the hora to an Irish jig without missing a beat.

When Senator Carl Levin's daughter Erica married Richard Fernandez, the ceremony included both Jewish and Portuguese Christian traditions. The music at the reception was jazz, klezmer, and Brazilian folk music.

An African-American couple in Washington, D.C., wanted to honor the groom's Nigerian heritage. They wore traditional Western attire to the wedding but changed into Nigerian garb for the reception. A Caribbean steel band started the reception and an African deejay finished it.

A recent bride of Chinese ancestry chose to carry a red bouquet with her Western white wedding dress, marrying the two traditions. She included a tea ceremony at her wedding reception. The cocktail reception began with firecrackers and a lion dance. But at the reception, the guests dined on paella and fajitas. Neither the bride nor the groom had Spanish roots—the groom just loved the food.

Another Asian bride's family met with a fortune-teller to pick a lucky wedding date. Guests were given small boxes with fortune cookies. But the wedding celebration was decidedly Moroccan. The reception was held in a Berber-like tent and another tent filled with floor pillows encouraged guests to lounge around, snack on fruits and nuts, and sip exotic teas. For their first dance together, the bride and groom chose a Cuban love song from the Buena Vista Social Club.

There are lots of charming traditions that can add to your daughter's wedding. Feel free to borrow any of them.

In Bermuda, the wedding cake is topped by a tree sapling that can be planted in the newlyweds' garden.

In France, couples drink from a two-handled cup called a *coupe de marriage.*

At Latino weddings, godparents *(padrinos)* often serve as sponsors, helping to pay for the wedding and providing moral support for the couple throughout the wedding process.

In Mexico, the guests form a heart-shaped ring around the bride and groom before the first dance.

In Japan, the couple takes nine sips of sake. They are husband and wife after the first sip.

According to theknot.com, at a traditional Russian wedding, the best man is assigned to protect the bride from evil spirits. This is no casual assignment. He has to walk counterclockwise three times around the bridal entourage, holding a religious icon. While he is making his rounds, other members of the bridal party crack whips, fire guns, and make as much noise as possible. Then the best man kneels in front of the bride and scratches the ground with his knife, cursing anyone or anything in the vicinity that might want to harm the bride, including but not limited to ex-girlfriends of the groom.

Unfortunately, wedding parties and wedding guests with firearms can have unintended consequences. A few years ago, the Associated Press reported that wedding guests accidentally shot down a small plane while protecting the bride from evil spirits.

Reality Check #21

TO BAGPIPE OR NOT TO BAGPIPE?

1. The bagpipe is strictly a Celtic instrument. If all of the alleged descendants really had ancestors on the Celtic Islands, these islands would have sunk into the sea a century ago.

2. The bagpipes are always played by a man in a skirt. Either his legs are so awful they shouldn't be on display or they are so awesome that they put the groom to shame and inspire the mother of the bride to jump him during the cocktail reception.

3. The truth is that there are few sounds on earth more mournful than that produced by bagpipes. Players of the pipes often need plenty of liquid fortification before they can bear to begin playing. It boggles the mind to think of any mother of the bride picking a pickled piper if she is under no ethnic obligation to do so.

22

THE WEDDING NAZI'S GUIDE TO BRIDAL ETIQUETTE

You thought you knew your daughter. You accepted the fact that she lived like a slob, dined on leftover lo mein cold from the carton, and wore jeans cut so low they barely covered her navel ring. Then, shortly after her engagement was announced, you heard a familiar voice demanding finger bowls and a palate-cleansing sorbet between courses at the wedding reception.

I remember that I had my moment of bridal madness. As soon as I got engaged, I bought a stack of bridal magazines. It was 1968 and I was living in New York's bohemian Greenwich Village with unmatched furniture and unwashed dishes. As soon as I became a bride-to-be, I started channeling Emily Post.

That is what has happened to the slob you know and love. She too has started reading bridal magazines. Somewhere in every issue, buried between ads for bridal gowns, silver, china, and honeymoon beaches, are the guides to proper wedding etiquette. Chances are your daughter also signed on to theknot.com and the other wedding Web sites with their own etiquette experts. You probably contributed to the indoctrination process, too—you bought her one of the pastel loose-leaf wedding planners packed with its own "dos" and "don'ts" for the big day.

You aren't immune to etiquette angst either. You've always been confident in your ability to know right from wrong and act accordingly. You don't wrestle old ladies for the last seat on a crowded bus or show up for church in cutoffs and dirty sneakers. You are so sensitive to offending others that if you bump into a blank wall, you say "excuse me." But as soon as your daughter got engaged, you started consulting etiquette books, convinced that you would commit some outrageous act that would shame your entire family in front of the in-laws.

If by some incredible fluke, neither you nor your daughter caught the etiquette bug on your own, one of the Wedding Nazis will make sure you get a dose. It will usually be someone you are paying for the privilege of insulting you.

You like daisies? The florist will sniff as if you suggested skunk weed.

You want to omit British spellings on your invitation? The invitation lady will make it clear that, under those circumstances, the Queen would not deign to attend.

Your daughter wants to walk herself down the aisle? The wedding planner will imply that this is obviously a sign of uncaring parents.

No aspect of wedding behavior is ignored by the army of white glove experts whose whole *raison d'être* is to make us mere mortals feel like uncivilized idiots who were raised by wolves.

Here is a sample of the wedding wisdom dispensed by the bridal etiquette experts in magazines, on Web sites, and in wedding guides:

Can the mother of the groom wear any color she likes?

Not according to one etiquette expert. The mother of the groom should stay away from dresses in the white, ivory, or champagne color family, lest anyone in attendance get the mistaken impression that the groom's mama sees the bride as a rival for his affections. She better not wear black either since black suggests mourning (loss of a son), funerals, and doom. And woe to the mother who chooses red or another bright color. She's showing her defiance and her flamboyance.

Where do they get this stuff? If the bride is perfectly happy with the mother of the groom in ecru, ebony, or scarlet, no one else should raise an objection. Nobody is likely to mistake the groom's mother for the bride. And the cut of her jib is far more important than the color in conveying her celebratory mood. The mother in black will look svelte rather than sad—unless she sobs dramatically throughout the ceremony. In such cases she could be wearing sea green or blush rose and she still wouldn't look happy.

"My fiancé's niece will be 9 years old by the time of our wedding (she is 7 now) and has her heart set on being our flower girl for almost two years. I have always thought that flower girls are very young (3 and 4 years old), and I was wondering if 9 years old is too old to be a flower girl?

The wedding expert decreed that 9 was too old, "unless she is small in size and can pass for younger."

I doubt that anyone seeing a 9-year-old coming down the aisle would ask to see her birth certificate. Etiquette experts sometimes invoke arbitrary rules that no bride should be forced to follow.

My parents are divorced (both have remarried) and relations between them are rancorous. My father and stepmother are paying for the wedding. How should our invitations read, and where should I seat both couples?

The white glove wizard who tackled this one opined that everyone's name should go on the invitations. As for seating the battling exes, the bride was advised to ascertain if all would agree to be on their best behavior. If so, all could sit together in the front row. Otherwise, the parents should be seated in separate rows with a buffer row between them. Presumably, the people seated in the buffer row should be prepared to referee any altercation or, if necessary, forcibly remove the offending party. At the reception, the bride was advised to establish separate (and separated) tables for the parties of the two couples.

If only holding an etiquette book over their heads would frighten families into submission! Alas, if love and consideration for their daughter, the bride, doesn't motivate them to behave, nothing in an etiquette book is going to keep these parents in line. Of course, you wouldn't dream of making a scene and spoiling your daughter's big day. But if your ex or any other relation seems bent on doing so, the bride must weigh the merits of having them there against their predilection for bad behavior. Merely throwing the etiquette book at them won't do the job.

Your daughter can take some comfort from the fact that weddings—and marriages—can survive even blatant bad behavior. Letitia Baldrige was Jacqueline Kennedy's White House Social Secretary. Baldrige inherited the mantle of etiquette doyenne from Amy Vanderbilt in the 1970s. She tells of a wedding where the father of the bride, emboldened by a few glasses of celebratory champagne at the reception, slugged the mother's new husband. The bride's father did help to revive his victim and publicly apologized. He even led a toast to "someone who has finally made the bride's mother a very happy woman."

Our invitation reads "Adult Reception." A friend just told me she is bringing her kids. How do I explain to her that I don't want children at my wedding? Or do I just let her bring them?

The etiquete expert stated that "Adult Reception" on the invite should have been enough to keep kiddies away. If a friend ignored that overt message and responded for herself and her little darlings, the bride was advised to call and explain why she was discouraging young guests. She should be prepared to justify her decision, the advice giver said. Mentioning the breakables at the reception site or the late hour of the celebration might motivate the friend to leave her children at home.

If you ask me, anyone who ignores a written instruction to leave their children home is not going to respond to subtle hints. This is an ideal opportunity for the mother of the bride to save her daughter from a confrontation. You can call the friend and impress upon her that no matter how charming and well behaved her offspring are, they will not be welcome at the wedding.

You can offer to arrange a babysitter, but the kind of people who want to inflict their kids on others are often the same people who wouldn't dream of letting a babysitter near their precious children. These are the same people who seem deaf and blind when their children run through the aisles on airplanes, screaming at the top of their lungs, or throw sugar packets over the booths in restaurants.

I am a bridesmaid in a friend's wedding. We have been friends since high school and I was very excited to be part of her day. When I got my invitation in the mail, I found out that I was not allowed to bring a date. I have been dating my boyfriend for three years now, and I do not understand why he was not included in this day. As a bridesmaid who is putting a lot of time, effort, and money into her day, I would think so. What should I do?"

The bridal magazine etiquette columnist advised the bridesmaid to write a letter to the bride, explaining how important her boyfriend is in her life. However, if the bride is not swayed, the bridesmaid has no choice but to attend alone.

This a classic case of old etiquette rules clashing with new romantic realities. Traditionally, only a fiancé was entitled to an invitation. Now that people wait longer before marrying, relationships can be serious without the "official" sanction of a formal engagement. Same-sex couples may be lifelong partners without exchanging rings. Brides—and mothers of brides—who stubbornly cling to outdated etiquette risk hurting the feelings of people close to them.

Etiquette is often invoked when there's a numbers crunch—too many would-be guests and not enough room in the hall or in the budget to accommodate them. I know of several young men and women who were invited solo to weddings and they really resented it. Shouldn't they have understood the bride's dilemma? No. It is not the guest's job to make the bride's life easier.

How can you let the guests know that you and your beloved are working toward a down payment on a house?

The manners maven at a Web site for women replied that she was opposed to the idea of a wedding as a fund-raiser, but the bride and groom could tell family members and their wedding party.

Wedding etiquette experts get a lot of questions from greedy brides. When a bride asked if she could include on the wedding invitation that wedding gifts should be sent to the couple's home, Peggy Post slapped her smartly on the wrist with her white gloves. Ms. Post replied in *In Style Weddings:* The thoughtful guest sends a gift to the bride's home before the wedding. In some communities, however, it's also customary to bring gifts to the wedding. Nevertheless, it would be impolite to make mention of gift delivery arrangements in your invitations, since it would seem as if you are focusing more on gifts than on the invitees. So let friends inform guests by word of mouth that advance delivery of gifts would be most appreciated.

Far be it from me to disagree with the heiress of Emily Post, but she let that bride off easy. Anyone who looks a gift wok in the mouth, so to speak, deserves to get a lump of coal instead.

This is the toughest subject for the mother of the bride. This is a case of the bride acting atrociously. The bride who posed this particular question is an amateur when it comes to imperious demands. Some brides treat wedding gifts as the price of ad-

mission to the wedding and want to dictate where the gift should be purchased and how much it should cost.

All of the etiquette columns in bridal publications are filled with outrageous questions from brides, operating under what author Judith Martin, aka Miss Manners, calls "the appalling belief that a wedding is the bride's day during which she is permitted to act like a tyrant." She is particularly offended by brides who treat their nuptials as show business. In *Miss Manners on Painfully Proper Weddings,* she writes, "Capturing the event on film for another audience is treated as superseding any need to accommodate those actually present. . . . Guests may be shoved aside or made to endure long blank waits, or cast without warning as extras, if the film script calls for candid reaction interviews."

Under these circumstances, guests could demand the rights of actors with speaking parts—full makeup, scale wages, and retakes if the camera catches you chewing with your mouth open.

Can you use etiquette to keep your darling daughter from turning into Bridezilla? It's worth a try. Bring out the etiquette book to bolster your argument that yes, she does have to invite aunts and uncles even if she dislikes them, and yes, she does have to invite the groom's sister to be in her wedding party, even if she wears coke-bottle glasses, has a hairy mole the size of Rhode Island, and will "spoil" the wedding pictures.

On the other hand, there is no rule of etiquette that requires the bride to invite her sister to be the maid of honor or to include all of her female cousins in the wedding party.

You need to think like a lawyer. As one attorney once told me, "If the law is on your side, argue the law. If the facts are on your side, argue the facts. If neither the law nor the facts are on your side, bang your fist on the table." Better yet, hit the bride upside the head with the etiquette book.

Common courtesy will take you further than all of the etiquette books. However, a guide to wedding etiquette can help you figure out how to word the wedding invitation, who walks where in the wedding procession, and who stands where at the ceremony. You can also use it to justify the assignment of corsages and pews.

If the bride and groom decide to deviate from protocol, that is their perogative. Just be sure they tell that to the officiant, the musicians, and anyone else who needs to know. At one wedding, the deejay invited the bride and her father up for their traditional dance. However, the bride was much closer to her stepfather and had planned to do the father-daughter dance with him instead. When her father stepped forward to dance with her, she felt trapped. She danced a few bars with her biological father, then sought out her stepfather to finish the dance.

Another bride was escorted down the aisle by both her father and her stepfather. At still another ceremony, the groom was escorted by his best friend—his dog.

Unthinkable? Unheard of?

At the very moment you are swearing that something "isn't done," someone, somewhere, is doing it.

Reality Check #22

10 THINGS THAT ARE STILL TABOO AT WEDDINGS— OR OUGHT TO BE

1. Actually objecting when the minister asks if there are any objections

2. Inviting yourself or bringing an uninvited guest

3. Snickering when the bride vows "for richer, for poorer"

4. Whispering "it's all downhill from here," as the happy couple comes down the aisle

5. Drinking so much that you don't remember dragging the bride's grandmother onto the dance floor to tango

6. Insisting that the band play the macarena

7. Complaining that the groom's family served better food at his bar mitzvah

8. Smashing the wedding cake into the bride's face

9. Calling the groom "whipped" because he didn't smash the wedding cake into the bride's face

10. Counting the wedding checks before all of the guests leave the reception

THE LIST

Your daughter, the bride, believes that her wedding is all about love.

Your husband, the father of the bride, believes the wedding is all about money.

Both are dead wrong. A wedding is all about numbers. How many people can you squeeze into a historic ballroom without inciting the fire marshall? How many drinks can you serve without breaking the bank?

Before you are through planning the wedding, you will learn to juggle numbers better than a crooked CPA working for Tony Soprano.

The process starts with the preliminary list—the people you, your daughter, her intended, and his family think must be invited to the wedding. The groom won't really focus on this until after baseball, football, soccer, basketball, golf, or lacrosse season. But the women in his life will start on their lists immediately.

In truth, you won't discuss the list with the in-laws until much later, when you've figured out just how big the wedding will be. You wouldn't want to raise false expectations—the bride may decide she wants a small wedding, limited to immediate family.

More likely, she will want a wedding limited to the immediate time zone.

The first version of the guest list will include everyone you, your husband, and your daughter have ever shared a blood tie, a neighborhood, a classroom, an office, or a zip code with. Hopefully, you'll discover that some of these people have changed their names, changed their addresses, divorced, died, or otherwise made themselves unavailable.

Even with a few dropouts, you'll soon realize that short of renting Yankee Stadium for the wedding and mortgaging grandchildren to be named later, you won't be able to invite everyone on your preliminary list.

Judith Martin, aka Miss Manners, advises families to invite everyone they want and divide the catering budget by that number. If that means the guests eat pretzels and drink punch, so be it! Miss Manners is such a font of wisdom about human be-

havior that I hate to differ with her. But on this issue, we part ways. There is a maximum number of people your wedding location and your budget can accommodate. There is a minimum repast you can provide for them. How do you apportion those maximums and minimums? To invite or not to invite, that is the question.

Years ago, the bride's family hosted the wedding and doled out the invitations. Many of us remember our own weddings as a roomful of adults, most of whom we barely recognized. One bride recalls that her mother told her she could not invite any friends who weren't in the wedding party. "If they aren't close enough to be bridesmaids, they can't be very good friends," her mother decreed.

Most brides and grooms would not tolerate such high-handed treatment today. The wedding bills are split more equitably and so are the guest lists. Even when the bride's family does pay for the entire wedding, you cannot hog the guest list. The bride and groom are probably older and have more friends and colleagues to invite. Limiting the groom's family to a handful of guests while you wine and dine your furnace repairman and that nice woman at the frame shop will not bode well for future family harmony.

List management gets even more complicated when there are divorced and remarried parents involved. As mentioned earlier, we divided our list into four equal parts: a fourth for our family, a fourth for Tony's family, a fourth for Meredith, and a fourth for Tony. Tony's parents are divorced and each has remarried. We never asked how they apportioned their allotted invitees.

The rule of thumb used to be that 20 percent of the invited guests will be unable to attend. Now wedding planners estimate the number is closer to 10 percent. The more advance notice you give guests and the more attractive you make the event, the smaller your percentage of regrets is likely to be.

In the months ahead, you will agonize over the list. This is the part of wedding planning that nobody talks about. Virtually every bride and every mother of the bride has a story about the ones who got away—the friends who didn't make the final list, the people you cringe to see afterward because they expected to be invited and you expected to invite them.

"I avoid some friends in the supermarket now," one mother confessed. "They knew Allyson her whole life. I never dreamed I wouldn't be able to invite them. But Allyson had so many friends, we didn't have room for all of mine."

I have been both the uninvited and the

uninviter, and neither is a happy role to play. It doesn't help to tell friends that they were the first runners-up, ahead of Aunt Martha and the podiatrist.

So, you take hold of your ideal list and you start cutting. First to go are the children. This is not a major sacrifice. Few people want a bunch of overtired, overstimulated kids running rampant through their reception.

Then you cross out relatives you wouldn't recognize on sight. Any friends you haven't seen in the past six months? Off the list. Now you just have to hope that they don't call to invite you to something.

Are you angry at anybody? Try to stay that way until after the wedding. This is no time to make new friends, join a new team, or take a new job. As it is, whole categories of cronies get erased in a single swipe. You

can't invite just a few members of the book club or the bowling league.

Before long, the negotiations between the wedding principals will begin. Does the bride's brother, aka your son, go on your list, the bride's list, or can you palm him off on the groom since he is also a groomsman? For that matter, does the bride go on her list or yours? Our magic number was 170. That meant we each got 42.5 guests. As I mentioned earlier, there were a few heated discussions about who was going to give up their half a guest so someone else could have a whole guest!

When all else failed, we resorted to the age-old compromise—the A-list and the B-list. We planned to invite the A-list 10 weeks before the wedding. If we got responses rapidly, we might get enough regrets to send out invites to the B-list 6 weeks in advance without anyone being the wiser.

It would have worked, too, if only in my

haste to get the invitations out, I hadn't mailed all of the invitations—both A-list and B-list—at the same time.

Meredith was understanding. Benjamin predicted disaster. For the two months before the wedding, we all had visions of the wedding party eating in the kitchen or sneaking extra guests past the atrium staff. Every time we got a "No," the mail carrier could hear me shouting "Yes!" in triumph.

My son-in-law offered to tell some of his friends not to show up. That didn't seem fair. So I did the only thing I could think of at the time. I'm not proud of this, but I may have subtly discouraged some people from coming. Well, maybe not so subtly.

When one of my colleagues regretted that he might be in Europe during the wedding weekend, I urged him not to change his plans. He thought he might be coming back in time. I warned him about airport delays and jet lag. Finally, I came clean.

"I invited too many people," I told him.

"Don't worry, it always works out," he assured me.

He went home that night and recounted our conversation to his wife. She got the message on the first try. The next day he promised me that they wouldn't come.

I needn't have worried. We ended up with a few last-minute cancellations and 163 people, well within the capacity of the room. But by the time we realized that we weren't over the limit, it was too late to go back to some of my friends and colleagues and encourage them to come.

How do you say, "I know we invited you and then, in effect, disinvited you, but we're really inviting you now!"

Reality Check #23

PLAYING THE NUMBERS

1. You have to put yourself on the list. You'll need a chair and a table and a place setting even though you swear you won't eat a bite.

2. Don't invite anyone because you assume he or she is too old, too sick, or too far away to attend. The person will probably make a miraculous recovery and make a reservation to fly in for the big day.

3. Don't try to save space by inviting anyone in a serious relationship without their en-amorata because they're not officially en-gaged. It is insulting to think you don't take a couple seriously unless jewelry is ex-changed.

4. This should go without saying, but gay couples should be treated as you would treat straight couples. You can't invite one without the other.

5. If close friends or relatives have had a nasty divorce and you don't want to take sides, invite them both and seat them at opposite sides of the room. If you are worried about an emotional outburst, sit someone near each of them who can sit on the offending party before they start a scene.

24

THE DUKE AND DUCHESS OF BROOKLYN REQUEST . . .

There are two schools of thought about wedding invitations: the proper-form school and the free-form school. If you ascribe to the first, there are any number of etiquette books that outline, in laborious detail, the exact language you must use to invite guests to your daughter's wedding. Here's one example:

When the bride's parents are divorced but her mother has not remarried, the mother uses her given, maiden, and married names on the first line, separate from her husband's, as follows:

Mrs. Marian Never-Again Blaine

Mr. Stanley Livingston Blaine

request the honour of your presence at

the marriage of their daughter

Samantha

The invitation can get a little crowded when the parents of both bride and groom are listed and when both sets of parents have divorced and remarried such as in the following example:

Mr. and Mrs. Henry Gotrocks

Mr. and Mrs. Steven Spendthrift

request the honour of your presence at

the marriage of their daughter

Goldilocks

to

Jonathan Livingston Seigel,

son of

Mr. and Mrs. Thomas Hawk

Mr. and Mrs. Montauk Seigel

You will note the British spelling of "honour." According to the Etiquette Nazi who helped us select invitations for Meredith's wedding, the fact that we declared our independence from Great Britain a mere two centuries ago does not relieve us of the obligation to employ the King's English on formal occasions.

"Honour of your presence" indicates that wedding vows will be exchanged in a house of worship. If the ceremony will be held in a secular setting, you can request "the pleasure of your company."

Meredith was married in an ecumenical atrium, thus freeing us from offending the Queen and the empire.

Etiquette expert Letitia Baldrige is a proponent of proper form. In *Letitia Baldrige's New Manners for New Times,* Baldrige not only provides the correct language for invitations, which should be a double-fold with the text engraved on the first page, but she also offers step-by-step instructions on inserting the invitation into the envelope. And here you've been shoving bills into envelopes for years—it's a wonder the phone company didn't return your check for faulty stuffing!

Tissue paper used to be included because the engraving ink might not be totally dry when the invitation was inserted in the envelope. Inks now dry fast enough so that tissue is no longer necessary, but many invitations still come with tissue because it looks elegant. Baldrige does not address the issue of inside and outside envelopes, assuming that even we ill-mannered peasants understand the need for both.

If you ascribe to the proper-form school, you will have no problem finding the right white or ecru stock and a type style suitable for the occasion. (Heavy, 60-pound paper, please. Support your local post office.)

The typefaces for formal invitations all have English-sounding names—Belgrave, Hamilton, Mayfair, Parsipal, London Script, Saint James, Windsor, and so on.

I do know at least two brides who spent more time picking a paper and a typeface for the invitation than on any other wedding detail. One bride rejected a font because she didn't like the M. The groom's name was Michael. Another pored through book after book of invitations looking for just the right square design.

An obsession with invitations is not necessarily a bad thing. Encourage the bride to compare typefaces to her heart's content and let you know when she has picked one. It will keep her mind off stickier issues like where you are going to sit the battling bachelor uncles who don't speak to each other or any other members of the family.

Just remind the bride that invitations must be ordered at least four months in advance so they can be addressed and mailed at least six to eight weeks in advance. If you hope to get responses early enough to invite replacements if you get any turndowns, move this timetable up a few weeks.

How many invitations should you order? Most invitations come in multiples of 25. We were advised to err on the side of ordering more than we needed, since reprinting can be costly. We're thinking about papering a powder room with the extra invitations and envelopes we have left over.

Proper form requires that invitations be hand-addressed and hand-stamped—no postage meters please. You can hire a calligrapher or write them yourself in your finest handwriting—or enlist a relative or bridesmaid who writes clearly.

We found a machine calligrapher who was cheaper and faster than a person with a pen. She had a font with enough flourishes and curlicues to impress our guests. She also calligraphed the placecards.

The post office stocks a number of stamps featuring birds, flowers, and love themes appropriate for wedding invitations. Just be sure you put on enough postage. It isn't just the weight that counts—the postal service charges a premium for oversize or odd-size envelopes.

Some brides feel strongly about having the stamps hand-cancelled, so those ugly cancellation lines don't mar the appearance of the outside envelope. You may need to call several post offices to find a location in your area where they do hand-cancelling. There is no extra charge, but it is best to go at an off-hour, so that you are not attacked verbally or physically by other postal patrons in line behind you waiting to mail one letter.

Call me revolutionary, but I felt very strongly about two invitation issues. We would not use British spellings, and we would not use two envelopes. The practice of using two envelopes made sense when invitations were delivered by stagecoach and often arrived splattered with mud. Since it was unlikely that Meredith's wedding invitations would be conveyed by the Pony Express, that was not a consideration.

Meredith wanted invitations on colored stock, and she commissioned me to come up with original wording. That put us squarely in the free-form school of wedding invitations. The invitations she picked were pale green with a faint white design of leaves in the center. As long as the names were spelled right and the who, what, where, when, and why were clear, we could explore lots of possibilities.

Her invitation read:

Leslie and Benjamin Milk

delight in inviting you

to celebrate the marriage

of their daughter

Meredith Balmuth

to

Anthony Todd Zaslav

We know a mother of the bride who hand-painted 200 invitations and place-cards. You can send beribboned and be-raffiaed invitations. Designs in a rainbow of colors or featuring hearts, flowers, cupids, wedding bells, entwined rings, and decorative borders are popular. Any combination of participants can do the inviting:

Goldilocks Gotrocks

and

Jonathan Livingston Seigel

together with their parents

Goldilocks Gotrocks

and

Jonathan Livingston Seigel

invite you share our joy

Henry and Harriet Gotrocks

Stephanie and Steven Spendthrift

Thomas and Tabitha Hawk

Marilyn and Montauk Seigel

request the honour of your presence

as their children

Goldilocks

and

Jonathan

are united in marriage

Goldilocks Gotrocks

and Jonathan Livingston Seigel

invite you to share

a day of happiness

as they begin a life of love

Some cynics may have a problem with sappy, sentimental wording on wedding invitations. I prefer simple expressions of joy, but if the bride and groom don't suffer from sugar overload, they are free to indulge in gushiness. Such sentiments as "Dreams do come true" and "Today I marry my best friend" certainly convey the couple's enthusiasm for the event.

It is helpful to indicate how you expect guests to dress for the wedding. Our invitation lady advised us to put "black tie optional" on the invitation. "Otherwise people will come in sports shirts and chinos," she said.

More and more invitations call for "black tie," "black tie optional," or "black tie preferred." There are two reasons for this. First, considering the escalating cost and elaborateness of weddings, it only seems fair for guests to dress as if they were attending a state occasion. Second, casual dress is so much the norm now that people show up at the opera in shorts and tank tops. "Black tie optional" is a classy way of saying "shirt and shoes required."

Can you send e-mail invitations? According to most protocol pooh-bahs, if you pose this question, you should be remanded to remedial etiquette class immediately. "Sending an invitation by e-mail or fax is easy but ugly and robs the wedding of its feeling of importance," according to Letitia Baldrige. Peggy Post of the Emily Post Institute concedes that an e-mail invitation is acceptable if the couple would have been phone-calling invitations or for last-minute and casual weddings.

Tacky as they may seem, e-mail invitations have one advantage: It is very easy for invitees to respond to them. Guests are increasing lax about responding to all invitations, even for weddings.

Once you put your invitations in the mail, the waiting game begins. The responses trickle in while you bite your nails wondering how many people will attend. It is particularly nerve-racking when you have a limit on the number of guests and, if someone cannot come, you'd like the chance to invite someone else to fill their chair.

Putting a "please respond by" date on the response card and stamping the response envelope so that the guest doesn't have to hunt for a stamp doesn't seem to make much difference.

If the response date has passed and you haven't heard, whoever knows the guest best can call and ask if they are coming. Won't this be embarrassing for the invitee?

I certainly hope so.

Reality Check #24

THE LANGUAGE OF LOVE

What if you can't agree on the look or the language of the invitations? In one case, the mother of the bride wanted a very religious Hindu text. The couple had agreed to a short religious ceremony, but they wanted secular invitations. The mother sent her version to her friends, and the bridal couple sent a different invitation to theirs. The separate but equal approach worked for them.

25

IF IT'S THURSDAY,
THIS MUST BE SOFTBALL

Guess who's coming to dinner . . . and breakfast . . . and to the park for a softball game . . . and to the golf course for 18 holes while the bridal party is off getting updos and French manicures? Your out-of-town wedding guests.

Far-flung friends and families often travel great distances at considerable expense to get to weddings these days. We mean to get together more often, but all too often, we need the impetus of a wedding, a bar mitzvah, or a funeral to spend time with the people we love. In fact, we often skip the good times, but guilt gets us together for the bad times. Be glad that nobody had to die to get all of your sibs in the same room!

For friends of the bride and groom, weddings are the new high school and college reunions. It's a chance for their personal rerun of *The Big Chill, St. Elmo's Fire,* or *Friends.* The happy couple wants to spend a lot of time with their friends both before and after the actual wedding. They want to introduce their old friends to their new friends and each other. And they want lots of parties and gatherings to do it.

Your daughter may want to go to great lengths to show her friends the best your area has to offer. One Maryland bride insisted on an authentic crab feast for all of the wedding guests the night before her wedding. The tables were covered with newspaper and then the steamed crabs were strewn across the newspaper. Each guest received a wooden mallet, a nutcracker, and instructions to "dig in."

Guests who arrived in party clothes and those who have a problem eating anything that makes eye contact had some difficulty with the full Chesapeake crab experience.

The mother of the bride who was getting married in wild and wonderful West Virginia planned a hayride and a hoedown for all of the guests. Many were aging urbanites who had to purchase blue jeans for the occasion.

It is important to remember that guests are coming to celebrate, not to emigrate.

You don't need to go to extremes. In fact, you won't be thrown out of the mother-of-the-bride union if you decide to interpret your role as the hostess of the wedding and nothing but the wedding. But these days out-of-towners do have expectations.

They'll expect you to recommend a place to stay and plenty of places to play. In addition, most brides and their families welcome wedding travelers with gifts, goodies, and guides and try to make sure they have a good time for the whole weekend of the wedding.

You'll be grateful to know that you aren't responsible for all of the activities and expenses. In most cases, wedding guests pay for their own accommodations, meals, and incidentals. A wedding weekend isn't like summer camp—you don't have to fill your guests' every waking hour with activities. They'll be happy to have free time to hang out with each other.

That said, I have noticed that a small number of couples are actually renting summer camps for their wedding festivities and scheduling a series of camp activities for all the guests to enjoy. You may need to intervene on behalf of guests whose childhood experiences at summer camp were less than idyllic. I, for one, break out in hives at the mere mention of "bug juice" or "color war."

Let's assume that you are hosting a wedding in normal surroundings and under normal circumstances. The groom's family generally hosts the rehearsal dinner the night before the wedding. Rehearsal dinners often include out-of-towners as well as the wedding party. Strict constructionists may not agree, but spouses, significant others, dates, escorts, or companions of wedding party members are usually included, too.

Other friends and relatives can host a bridesmaids' luncheon, a postwedding brunch, or any other gathering for the wedding party and guests. You should welcome these offers of hospitality. You don't have to mastermind every moment of the wedding weekend. You'll have enough to do managing the main event.

As soon as the wedding date is set, you should check out hotels near your wedding venue. Out-of-towners aren't the only ones who may want to stay in a hotel on the night of the big bash. The bride and groom, the wedding party, and you yourself may want to be close to the action. Local guests who want to drink more than a glass of wine may also prefer to stay at a hotel near the wedding venue rather than driving themselves home.

You and the bride can pull together a rough estimate of the number of rooms you'll need. Some mothers of brides scout

out a few different hotels and inns in different price ranges. That way, young friends of the bride and groom can decide on accommodations that fit their budgets. However, if you reserve a block of rooms in one hotel, you'll get a better room rate, and you may get the bridal suite or other amenities as part of the package.

It pays to go to the hotel's general manager and negotiate. Most hotels operate like airlines—room rates fluctuate like the stock market. There are corporate rates, senior citizen rates, group rates, in-season rates, off-season rates, and all kinds of improbable arrangements. There's probably a rate for redheads and a different rate for brunettes.

We booked a block of rooms and the groom's family also hosted the morning-after brunch at the hotel. Because we booked more than 20 room-nights (some people stayed more than one night) and we held a catered event in the hotel, we were able to get a complimentary suite for two nights, a room for the wedding rehearsal, and vans to transport guests to the wedding venue as part of our hotel package. We also got a dirt-cheap room rate.

You may have to sign a contract to guarantee a certain number of rooms. Often the hotel will give you a room reservation card to send with your invitations. If guests call for reservations, they should tell the hotel that they are part of the wedding so they can take advantage of the great room rate you arranged.

Remember all the goodie bags you packed for your kids' birthday parties? You'll get to do it again for your daughter's wedding. Out-of-town guests have come to expect welcome packages from the bride when they check into the hotel.

The goodies often reflect the theme of the wedding or the city where it is held. I've seen welcome baskets with Chesapeake Bay seasoning, Virginia peanuts, New Orleans pralines, and San Francisco's Ghirardelli chocolates. A welcome to a beach-front wedding might include flip-flops and suntan lotion. Guests to a woodsy wedding might find trail mix and bug repellent in their goodie bags.

Hospitality packages usually include a welcome letter to tell guests about the schedule of events and transportation arrangements. You can stick in Chamber of Commerce brochures about tourist attractions and museums that your guests might like to visit. Along with some snacks, these goodie bags almost always include bottled water—even in cities like New York, where you can drink the water. Heaven forbid that any wedding guest should be forced to drink actual tap water!

You don't have to go to great lengths to hunt down local delicacies. Just because they're in Boston doesn't mean your guests want to eat baked beans. They'd rather have chocolate, chips, and if you are really desperate, some healthy snack.

I was lucky. The groom's mother, Susan Goldstein, has a gift business. She put together the welcome bags for all of the guests who stayed at the hotel. I contributed a copy of the current *Washingtonian* magazine. Meredith and Tony contributed bottles of their wedding water. Susan added a welcome letter, chocolates, and other goodies.

Bridal experts suggest that the welcome goodies be packaged in baskets, flowerpots, and other imaginative vessels. Remember that your guests have to pack these gifts for the trip home. Try packing a flowerpot in a suitcase! Don't tell Martha Stewart, but bags work much better.

At some point during the wedding marathon, you may start to wonder why you are doing so much to entertain out-of-town guests. Think how rare it is that you are all together. Then think of the alternative. You certainly didn't want them all staying at your house!

The morning after the wedding, many newlyweds want to join their guests for a farewell breakfast or brunch. This doesn't have to be a fancy, china-and-placecards affair. Everybody will welcome a chance to wear jeans or sweats, grab a paper plate, a cup of coffee, and a Danish, hang out for a while, and leave when they need to catch their plane or train home.

For the bride and groom, it's a chance to share a few more hours of wedding glory. For you, it's a chance to accept the compliments on a fabulous celebration. Enjoy the moment and take the credit. You've earned it.

Reality Check # 25

BITE YOUR TONGUE BEFORE YOU UTTER THESE WORDS

1. We've got an extra bedroom.
2. We've got room in our car.
3. Bring the baby. We'll find a sitter.
4. Bring the dog. We'll find a sitter.

GOTTA DANCE

Tough guys don't dance. Not-so-tough guys don't dance. The fact is that most guys don't dance—at least not when they are sober.

There are, of course, exceptions. Black guys often say only white guys can't dance. Some Latinos claim they can salsa all night long. But take a good look at couples on any dance floor. Most of the men are moving, but it is a stretch to call what they are doing "dancing."

If the music is slow, they are spread over their partner like peanut butter and their feet are shuffling. In fact, one man admitted that the only reason he danced in his youth was because it gave him a legitimate excuse to grab a girl and hold on for dear life.

If the music is fast, they are doing some combination of flailing arms, nodding heads, and stamping feet. It may not be pretty, but on a crowded dance floor when the lights are low, they can get away with it.

Most men do not admit they are terrible dancers. I once asked a group of guys whether they could dance. Their responses ranged from, "Sure, I can dance. Did somebody tell you I couldn't?" to "Dance? You mean move around?" to "I can dance with the mother of the bride if it's absolutely required."

Most women are so grateful to be on the dance floor that they will accept any reasonable facsimile. As long as our partners don't trip, tackle, or maul any of the other dancers in the process, we are happy.

At many parties and celebrations, when the joint starts jumping, the women get out on the dance floor and dance with each other. Girls grow up practicing dance steps in front of their mirrors and in front of their TV sets. They mimic moves they see on music videos. They start out dancing together, and they still have a much better time dancing together than with their husbands, lovers, or dates.

In the grand scheme of things, dancing doesn't rate up there with being able to cure cancer or create world peace. Nobody says of Abraham Lincoln, "He was a great president, but he couldn't mambo." Sure, it would be nice if the men in our lives were Patrick Swayze, John Travolta, or Savion Glover, but we'll settle for safe at any speed. Why do you think so many women close their eyes when they are out on the dance floor?

However, there are times in a man's life when he has to dance. He is expected to dance with his bride at their wedding reception. If he is lucky enough to have a daughter, he gets a second chance to dance with her at her wedding reception.

"Lucky" is not the word a man would use to describe the experience. He knows he not only has to dance but also has to dance in the spotlight with his whole world watching and both still and video photographers immortalizing the moment. This is enough to strike fear into the heart of the macho and the meek alike.

First dance, first. Philosophers and members of the clergy can wax eloquent on the idea of the first dance as the graceful first steps in a new life together. Most men will be happy if they don't fall on their faces.

There are several ways to approach the "first dance." Some couples just wing it. Some couples take ballroom dancing lessons. Some hire a choreographer to create a dance number with enough dips and twirls to wow the crowd. At one wedding, the bride changed into a red satin dress and the newlyweds performed a sizzling merengue to the "olés" of their guests.

Whichever approach your daughter and her groom embrace, it will help if they pick a danceable song. In theory, the bride and groom dance to "their song." That assumes they have a song and that this song has lyrics which, when played at the wedding, will not horrify most of the guests. Many songs with great lyrics don't make great dance numbers.

Such classics as "Ain't No Mountain High Enough" or "Baby Got Back" or "I've Got Friends in Low Places" have truly heartwarming lyrics but leave something to be desired as dance numbers.

Weaning the bride away from "our song" may not be easy. Let the lovebirds try dancing to it. Remind the bride that for the actual first dance she'll be going backward, wearing high heels and a long skirt. If he steps on her feet when they are both in sneakers, imagine how it's going to feel when he's wearing heavy black shoes and she's wearing her strappy wedding sandals.

If the couple doesn't have a special song or are willing to consider a danceable tune, you can direct them to the nearest wedding Web site where they'll find lists of great first-dance songs like "Wonderful World," the Elvis classic "Can't Help Falling in Love with You," "You Send Me," by Sam Cooke, and "You've Got a Friend," by James Taylor.

These songs are amenable to the time-tested "clutch-and-sway" method of dancing that even neophytes can master. All the bride and groom have to do is hug each other and sway back and forth. If the groom is feeling adventurous, he can extend one arm and allow the bride to twirl underneath it. Hamming it up helps. Then they can resume clutching and swaying.

To the reluctant dancer, a 3- or 4-minute song can seem like a Wagnerian opera. One way to shorten the actual dance part is to have the couple approach the dance floor from opposite sides of the room. They can use a good 20 seconds just reaching each other.

Many couples take a few dance lessons before the big day. Almost as many forget the lessons on the big day and return to the clutch-and-sway. This is preferable to the terror that overwhelms some grooms when they try to perform the carefully choreo-graphed number they practiced with the dance teacher.

I've been to a few weddings where I watched the groom counting and sweating, sweating and counting, as he went through his paces. It was downright painful. One groom had written the routine on his wrist, but the contortions of the dance made it impossible for him to eyeball the instructions.

At another wedding, the first dance was flawless. It should have been—the perfectionist bride required so many rehearsals for the swing-dance routine that the groom nearly begged off from both the dance and the wedding. He was a pretty good dancer, but he wasn't interested in becoming the King of Swing.

This same bride turned waltzing with her father into a similar production number. He went along with the program—the father of the bride can't jilt his own daughter!

In a long-running credit-card commercial, a teary-eyed father of the bride masterfully waltzed his daughter around the floor, grateful that he had the wherewithal to make her wedding dreams come true. This is rarely the case. The father of the bride is far more likely to be a middle-aged guy in an uncomfortable suit, trying not to step on his daughter's dress. Those tears in his eyes are his way of saying, "Help! I'm being held on this dance floor against my will."

Like many other parents of brides, we did not feel confident about the two exhibition dances. Benjamin was particularly panicked about his time in the spotlight. So we signed up for a dance class at the local recreation department six months before the wedding. It soon became clear that group lessons would not be enough. I had done a lot of dancing in my youth. Benjamin had done more clutching than swaying.

Two months before the wedding, we started taking private lessons. Our first teacher was a man. This posed a slight problem because at some point each pupil has to dance with the teacher. Benjamin, who felt awkward on the dance floor anyway, could not kick up his heels in this guy's arms. We switched to a female instructor and our dancing skills improved.

Why, you might ask, was Benjamin taking lessons with me when I was not going to be his partner in the spotlight at the wedding? He figured that once he mastered a dance with me, dancing with Meredith would be easy. She wouldn't even try to lead!

He did get through his dance, but it wasn't painless. He was ready to relinquish the floor after one chorus, but the bride prevailed on him to keep "dancing."

No one expects the father of the bride and his daughter to have a special song. But sometimes a childhood memory makes a song special. One bride danced with her father to the Muppet theme song. The most popular father-daughter songs are "Butterfly Kisses," by Bob Carlisle, "Daddy's Little Girl," by Kippi Brannon or Al Martino, and "Unforgettable," by Natalie Cole. You can't go wrong with the classics, such as "Moon River," "Sunrise, Sunset," and "What a Wonderful World."

All of these songs work with a waltz, a box step, or clutch-and-sway.

If the bride has both a biological father and a stepfather, she can choose to dance with one or the other or split a song between them. Or, if the situation is awkward, she can skip the father-daughter dance altogether. She'd probably rather dance with her girl-friends—and we all know that her dad(s) would be just as happy.

Reality Check #26

THE REAL DANCE LESSONS

Dance instructors will tell you that anyone who can walk can dance. They lie. Anybody who can talk can sing, too, but that doesn't mean you'd want to listen. Given that most men can't dance, here are a few simple rules for the first dance and the father-daughter dance.

1. Slow is better than fast—less opportunity for flailing, falling, and serious bodily injury.
2. Take a short cut. The longer the song, the greater the agony.
3. When in doubt, don't dip (see rule 1).
4. Practice doesn't necessarily make perfect.
5. A kiss covers a lot of awkward moves—but when the music stops, the kiss better stop, too.

Part 5

THE WEDDING

PLEASE BE SEATED

Arranging the tables at a wedding reception is like working on a trick jigsaw puzzle. You know that all the pieces are supposed to fit together, but they never do. There are always a few pieces left over. That's why the seating chart is often the last thing on the mother of the bride's to-do list. You think if you wait long enough, the tables will miraculously arrange themselves.

Do you have to assign tables? At an informal buffet reception, you can let guests seat themselves. But don't be surprised if some people save seats as if they were still riding on the school bus and others are left standing like losers in a game of musical chairs. Your guests will thank you if you spare them this embarrassment by assigning tables. Figuring out who sits where doesn't have to be a major headache.

The first decision is where to put the bride and groom. Should they sit with the wedding party or with the family or with both groups at a long head table? The easiest answer is none of the above.

More and more newlyweds are choosing to sit alone at a "sweetheart" table. This makes a lot of sense. For complicated families, it solves the problem of which set of parents get the bride and groom. As for the wedding party, the bridesmaids and groomsmen would rather sit with their significant others than isolated at a separate wedding party table. A sweetheart table also lets the bride and groom get up to make the rounds without deserting any of their nearest and dearest for long stretches of the evening.

When we got married, we sat on a long raised dais with both our attendants and our immediate families. All of our guests got to watch us chew. Sitting that way, we couldn't really talk to each other, so there was nothing to do but chew.

Traditionalists still call for a bridal table and a parents' table with strict guidelines about who sits where. Most brides are more interested in making the evening enjoyable for everyone than in observing protocol.

The next step is to hand off as much of the seating burden as you can to the other major players. Invite the bride, the groom, and the groom's mother to figure out the seating for their friends and colleagues.

Remember that most restaurants, hotels, and event facilities have tables in different sizes and shapes. Party planner extraordinaire Colin Cowie recommends using a mix of shapes and sizes to make the room more interesting. It also makes seating arrangements simpler when you don't have to fit all of your guests into neat little groups of 8 or 10.

Many wedding receptions have a kids' table or a singles' table. To me, this makes as much sense as sitting all of the blondes together or all of the lawyers together. Actually, the latter might make some sense, but most artificial groupings are uncomfortable for the guests.

If the kids don't know each other, they'd rather sit with their parents. Who wants to sit with a bunch of strangers just because they are about your size? Single people would rather sit with people they know, too, rather than making conversation with a bunch of people whose only common interest is the absence of a spouse. Use round tables and you won't need even numbers.

Some brides, awash in feelings of their own eternal love, see a wedding as a matchmaking opportunity. A wedding reception offers plenty of opportunities to introduce friends and relations. Almost any introduction is less awkward than (wink, wink) seating them side by side at dinner.

Guests are invited to have fun, not to find spouses, make new friends, or entertain your other guests. I say this as a friendly, outgoing person who often finds herself seated in Siberia, far from those I know and love, because I will talk to even the most taciturn tablemate. I have found myself seated with law partners who do not speak

to each other and ancient, hard-of-hearing aunts who rarely speak above a whisper. Meanwhile, I see the people I know laughing and carousing the night away. It isn't fair! At least not from where I sit!

Arranging the tables in the room can also be a challenge. Who sits near the bride and who sits near the kitchen? Most important, who faces the music? The answer to that one is easy—if you are struggling to find a group that can tolerate being near the band, that is an indication you'll need to ask the musicians to turn down the volume.

Finally, there shouldn't be a "bride's side" and a "groom's side" at the reception, as if the two families were warring countries that need a demilitarized zone between them.

These days many brides are naming their tables rather than numbering them—both to carry out the wedding theme and to keep guests from feeling that they didn't rank high enough to sit at a table with a low number. (Our caterer suggested reversing the expected order and putting table 1 farthest from the front.)

Naming tables after favorite songs, places the couple has visited, flowers, and so on, may make no sense to the guests, but if it pleases the bride and groom, there's nothing wrong with the idea. One bride chose to name her tables after the attributes that make a happy marriage—love, understanding, and so on. If I had been a guest, I would have wondered why I was placed at "balanced budget" rather than "hot sex."

Creativity is also running rampant in the design of "escort cards" that inform guests of their table assignments. Plain white cards with calligraphed names, lined up alphabetically on a skirted table, seems boring to many an imaginative bride or wedding planner. Now the cards "grow" on trees or the table numbers are iced onto cupcakes. Meredith's seating cards perched on a field of grass with flower petals strewn around them. (The grass was on a tabletop, so guests didn't have to kneel to find their numbers.)

While I have never observed guests yawning in boredom while looking for their seat assignments at a traditional display of white seating cards, I have no problem with a few ruffles and flourishes—as long they don't make it harder to find your table.

It helps if the names are written large enough so they can be read without fishing for your reading glasses. Finding your table assignment shouldn't require a scavenger hunt. At one wedding, the seat assignments were attached to the stems of yellow roses. At another they were taped to the bottom of the favors. In any case, guests shouldn't have to work so hard to find a place to sit down.

SEATING CHART STRATEGIES

1. It isn't enough to seat warring exes at separate tables. You need a three-table no-fly zone between them.

2. If you're worried that Uncle Fred will get tipsy, seat him farthest from the bar.

3. If you're worried about Grandma's reaction time, seat her closest to the ladies' room.

4. Never seat your boss with anyone who knew you when you were:

   a. protesting against the capitalist pigs
   b. still trying to make it as a rock star
   c. unemployed

28

WHEN BAD THINGS HAPPEN
TO GOOD WEDDINGS

You spend months planning the perfect wedding, agonizing over every detail. And then it rains. This is not the gentle rain that mists the air and sparkles on every flower. This is a monsoon. The wind howls, the thunder roars, and the tent totters under the weight of the rain.

This is a moment that separates the men from the boys and the women from the girls. Some get mad. Some get flip-flops.

When a summer storm threatened one outdoor wedding, the caterer said they would need to install an $11,000 wood floor in the reception tent or move the party indoors. The bride's father balked. Instead, he went to the mall and bought 100 pairs of rubber flip-flops in different colors, so the ladies wouldn't ruin their shoes on the wet grass. The guests loved it.

The tent did collapse under the weight of rainwater at another wedding. After the wedding party and guests climbed out, dripping and laughing, the caterer broke out extra champagne and a good time was had by all. Had it been a freezing-cold night or had anyone been injured, it might have been a different story.

Bad weather alone can't ruin a good wedding. Resilient families, brides, and grooms can salvage their celebrations. During power outages, couples have been married by candlelight. In the aftermath of a hurricane, a Carolina couple were married in shorts and high boots. One New York couple had to abandon their wedding plans when the city suffered a major blackout. They had planned a day-after party at the bride's family's summer home in Connecticut, so they moved the whole wedding there. However, their minister couldn't make it to Connecticut, and, since they had a New York marriage license, they had to be married in New York. They went to the minister's house, got married there, and then went off to Connecticut where an ordained friend did a second service in front of friends and family.

Letitia Baldrige tells about a wedding where lightning struck the church two hours before the ceremony and the church burned to the ground. The couple was married on schedule in the gymnasium next door, with flowers donated from neighboring gardens.

Some circumstances cannot be overcome by ingenuity and a positive attitude. If you have serious concerns about something going wrong, you should consider wedding insurance. Several companies, including Wedsafe, a division of Markel Insurance, and Fireman's Fund offer private event coverage.

A basic policy costs between $150 and $400 and covers postponement, cancellation, or additional expenses for circumstances beyond your control, such as inclement weather, sudden illness of the bride or groom, or loss or damage to the wedding attire or gifts. You'll also be covered if somebody drinks too much and gets hurt.

If there is a major technical problem with the wedding pictures or the video, the policy pays to restage and reshoot photos or videos, including reassembling the key participants.

You'll want to take out insurance as soon as you begin to spend money on the wedding. But be sure to read the fine print. One policy I read covered postponement if the bride or groom was in the military and was suddenly deployed. However, reservists weren't covered.

If the bride or groom backs out at the last minute, you'll have no recourse. Cold feet aren't covered.

Real tragedies are rare, but minor mishaps can take on tragic proportions if you or your daughter overreact to them. Most wedding planners carry their own emergency kits for spills, stains, rips, and other problems. If you're acting as your own wedding planner, create your own kit.

Toothpaste, baby powder, or chalk can hide a stain on a white wedding dress. A drooping hem can be mended on the spot with pins or two-sided tape. (At Meredith's wedding, the yarmulke kept slipping off the head of one of the groomsmen. I used two-sided tape to attach it to his bald spot.)

An emery board does double duty—to treat a broken nail or rough up the bottoms of slippery shoes. It doesn't hurt to have Band-Aids, breath freshener, hair spray, antiseptic, an Ace bandage, and over-the-counter remedies for headache, indigestion, and diarrhea, too.

Both you and the bride should bring an extra pair of shoes, in case a heel breaks or your feet hurt in your formal footwear.

The emergency kit should include the cell phone number of every vendor, including the officiant. They should have your cell phone number, too, in case they get stuck in traffic or something goes wrong.

What if one of the vendors is AWOL or can't deliver? Improvise. If the officiant fails to show on time, wedding planners advise switching the order of play and starting with the cocktail hour. As soon as the tardy marrying man or woman shows up, you can start the ceremony. You can also check the guest list—there may be a minister, judge, a justice of the peace, or an Internet-ordained officiant in the crowd who can do the honors.

If the limo doesn't show, hop in the car or call a taxi. If the musicians are missing, ask if any of the catering staff has a radio. At one wedding, the guests hummed the wedding march. If the baker drops the wedding cake, send someone out for cupcakes and pile them into an artistic pyramid. If the best man forgets the rings, lend him yours.

Remember, nobody else knows what was supposed to happen—unless you tell them. They'll never guess that you hadn't planned to dress the altar with a funeral wreath (presumably, you'll remove the banner that reads "In loving memory") or that you didn't intend for the bride's uncle to sing with the band.

One bride gave new meaning to the phrase "go with the flow." She had been unnaturally calm all day. Then, once she was all dressed in her gown with the train affixed and the veil in place, she felt the need to use the restroom. When she mentioned it, everybody ignored her. So she tried to ignore nature's call. The music started. The procession began. Finally, the bride shrieked, "I have to go—now." The wedding planner slowed the procession while the bride, the maid of honor, and the mother raced through the kitchen to the closest bathroom. The maid and mother held up the dress and the bride peed. Then the trio ran back through the kitchen, the maid of honor grabbed their bouquets, and the wedding proceeded as planned.

It doesn't hurt to be prepared for friends and family who are known to behave badly. You can't leave your hard-partying sister-in-law off the guest list, but you can alert the bartenders to water down her drinks before she starts dancing on the table. If the best man's toast goes from reminiscent to raunchy, signal the musicians or the deejay to strike up the band.

Bad behavior cannot always be anticipated. If a guest brings their baby to your adults-only wedding or brings an uninvited escort, you can't very well bar the door. If your ex objects to procession arrangements at the last minute, you have to do your best to mollify him without involving the bride. Yes, he's unreasonable—that's why you aren't married to him anymore. But this is your daughter's day, not the latest skirmish in your marital wars.

What if something serious goes wrong? If the bride and groom want the show to go on, you should do what you can to make it happen. If a guest or an attendant gets ill or injured, call 911, have someone stay with the injured party until help arrives, but don't cancel the wedding. That would only make the sick person feel worse.

Sometimes the presence of tragedy makes the idea of a wedding even more compelling. Many couples who had planned September weddings in 2001 considered canceling them after 9/11. When all the planes were grounded after 9/11, one bride and groom wanted to be with their families and friends to celebrate love and life in the face of tragedy. They drove across the country nonstop to get to their wedding in Washington, D.C. They created a telephone chain to let guests know the wedding was still on. And they got married.

Had either of them lost someone close in the World Trade Center or the Pentagon, it might have been a different story. In fact, one of the bridesmaids was the manager for the restaurant atop Tower One, but it was her day off.

It is not unusual for either the bride or the groom to come down with a case of pre-wedding jitters. I remember asking my best friend, Beth, to help me escape from the bridal suite. "I'm afraid that instead of saying 'I do,' I'm going to ask 'why you?'" I told her.

"I'm not going downstairs and telling your mother that the wedding is off," she shuddered. "I don't care if you get divorced next week. You're going through with this."

In my case, the jitters were just that. But if your daughter or her intended have serious doubts about the marriage, you don't want them to go through with the wedding just to avoid losing money or losing face.

Sometimes the engagement brings out differences that weren't obvious when the couple was merely dating. In one case, a religious difference that seemed minor during the courtship became a major issue before the wedding. The bride admitted that she secretly hoped the groom would convert. Another bride discovered that the groom wasn't just taking an occasional trip to Las Vegas. He had a serious gambling problem.

Sometimes circumstances change—one of the couple loses a job, starts drinking heavily, comes out of the closet, decides to join the Peace Corps in Africa, or falls in love with somebody else.

Sometimes the sheer momentum of the marriage process pushes a bride toward the altar before she is ready. "Women may find themselves feeling that if a man asks they have to say yes," Professor Tony Jurich of Kansas State University told a magazine. "In the moment, it's easy to believe that marriage automatically means happily ever after."

Once engaged, a young woman may feel that she cannot stop the speeding train that the wedding has become, even though she is no longer sure she wants to be married, let alone married to him.

Forget the deposits on the food and the flowers. Forget the pristine wedding gown hanging on your closet door. You don't want your daughter walking down the aisle when she'd rather be getting a root canal. And you don't want her marrying anyone who doesn't think he's the luckiest guy on earth to get her.

This is a true story—or true enough to have made the newspapers in Clemson, South Carolina, and Jay Leno's monologue. At the wedding reception for 300 guests, the groom got up on stage to thank everyone for coming. He announced that he had arranged a special "gift" for each guest: taped under each chair was an envelope containing a candid photo of the bride and the best man engaged in what could best be called a honeymoon rehearsal. The groom then cursed the bride and the best man and left the party. The next morning he had the marriage annulled.

The story smacks of urban legend. But if Aesop had written it, the moral would be: A broken engagement mends faster than a broken marriage.

Reality Check # 28

THE MOTHER OF THE BRIDE'S EMERGENCY KIT

1. Allergy medicine, pain reliever, antacids, antidiarrhea medication
2. Band-Aids for cuts and blisters
3. Blotting papers (for shiny noses)
4. Bobby pins (for fixing updos)
5. Bottled water for taking pills
6. Breath mints
7. Cell phone and all players' numbers
8. Chalk (to cover stains on bride's dress)
9. Clear nail polish (for runs in hose)
10. Crazy glue—for everything
11. Emery board
12. Extra cash, placecards and pen
13. Extra shoes for you and the bride
14. Eyedrops and hairspray
15. Hem tape
16. Makeup and mirror
17. Mini sewing kit with buttons
18. Safety pins and paper clips (they can double as cuff links)
19. Scotch tape
20. Seating chart
21. Sedatives
22. Snacks (in case the bride forgets to eat)
23. Spot remover
24. Static-cling spray
25. Straws (so bride can sip a drink without messing her makeup)
26. Tampons
27. Tissues
28. Toothbrush and toothpaste—can also be used on any stains in the wedding dress

Or just empty the contents of your medicine chest, cosmetics and toiletries shelves, and pantry into a suitcase and carry that.

MEMORIES ARE MADE OF THIS

Before Meredith's wedding, I planned to lose 20 pounds, get into shape, and find a dress that didn't shout "mother of the bride." I intended to plan the perfect affair without breaking the bank, breaking a sweat, or breaking out in hives. In my spare time, I'd do something about world peace.

By those standards, I was a flop. I lost maybe 10 pounds—okay, 6 or 7. I was in better shape than before, but hardly buff. I have since seen no fewer than five mothers of brides or grooms wearing versions of the dress I wore—so much for my quest for an atypical dress.

The wedding stayed within budget, but Benjamin would say that the budget was outrageous at the start. I lost most of my cool and plenty of sleep. Let's not even talk about world peace.

I can tell you all of the little things that went wrong on the wedding day:

The wedding ceremony was set up outside. It started to rain, so we moved it inside. The minute we put the canopy up inside, the rain stopped. I made an executive decision to stay inside, except for the cocktail hour, when almost everyone went outside. I had not anticipated that, so the chamber musicians stayed inside, playing to a mostly empty room.

While we were setting up, the assistant manager of the atrium casually mentioned that the parks department staff hadn't really expected us to abide by their maximum occupancy rule. All of our anxious head counts had been unnecessary. It was too late to do anything about it, but the irony was inescapable. Thanks to the people we invited who didn't come, the people we invited and then discouraged from coming, and the people we avoided in the months before the wedding because we thought we couldn't invite them, there were waiters at the wedding who knew more people there than Benjamin and I did.

The groomsmen raced down the aisle as if Jennifer Lopez were waiting for them at the altar. The chamber musicians were wonderful. It wasn't their fault that there was a momentary musical mix-up. The bride refused to move until she heard Pachelbel's Canon. Guests close to the back could hear us whispering, "Is that it? Do we go now?"

I never checked to see if the aisle was wide enough to walk three abreast. It wasn't. Benjamin and I walked Meredith down the aisle in vee formation.

We planned to put disposable cameras on every table. They were left in the limo by mistake.

As part of Jewish tradition, the bride and groom are lifted up on chairs and the guests dance around them. It is not a good idea to use folding chairs, which can collapse. We did.

Fortunately, nobody got hurt.

In the exuberance of the dance, the elastic on my skirt gave way and I had to grab it before it fell down to my knees. In case anyone missed it, they could see it on the video.

What took 16 months to plan was over in what felt like 16 minutes. Somehow Benjamin and I both missed the cutting of the cake.

But these are minor details.

Whenever I think about the wedding, I think of my son Jeremy at the rehearsal dinner, presenting the resurrected "Blankie" of my daughter's youth. My mother used to ask, "How long are you going to let her carry that thing? Is she going to take it to college?" In fact, she did, as her sorority sisters-turned-bridesmaids reminded her. Blankie is still in remarkably good shape for its age.

I think of the rare opportunity to see our far-flung family together. Our little brothers are now bigger than we are.

I think of standing under the canopy made by so many loving hands and hearing our daughter take the same Hebrew vows that we took—since none of us actually understands Hebrew, we have to take it on faith that we agreed to marry each other, not sacrifice a goat while standing on one foot and whistling "Dixie."

I think of Meredith dancing with her father to a song I used to sing to her: "Turn around and you're growing, turn around and you're grown, turn around and you're a young wife with a child of your own."

I think of gorging on wedding cake because the photographer and the videographer had gone home and it didn't matter anymore how I looked in my dress.

I think of a picture someone took of Benjamin and me. It was late in the evening, at the reception. We were sitting at our table with a lot of empty glasses in front of us. We were watching the maid of honor toast the bride and groom, and we were both smiling.

What were we smiling at? Survival. We made it through the chicken pox and allergy shots, the math tutors and the orthodonture, the times we were too tired to talk and the times we yelled ourselves hoarse over something the kids did or didn't do.

There is a lot of luck involved in parenting. When you get married, you wonder if your children will have his eyes or your hair. Then you look at some of your relatives and realize there's some very weird stuff swimming around in the gene pool.

Our kids got my overbite and Benjamin's flat feet, but, all in all, they got the best of both of our families.

Our kids survived more than just the slings and arrows of suburban childhood. They survived us—our ignorance, our impatience, our insistence on teaching them the lessons we learned from our own youth, even if they no longer applied to theirs.

And we lived long enough to see them both come shining through.

Reality Check # 29

WAS IT WORTH IT?

Absolutely.
Meredith says it was the best day of her life.

MOTHER OF THE BRIDE MOVIE GUIDE

TOP 20 INSTRUCTIONAL FILMS WITH IMPORTANT LESSONS FOR THE MOTHER OF THE BRIDE

American Wedding (2003) This film offers a vivid portrayal of gross, immature behavior by a prospective groom and his buddies. You have cause for alarm if you see any resemblance to your daughter's intended.

The Best Man (1999) Actor Taye Diggs offers a life lesson on how a wedding can stir up old grudges as well as old memories.

The Bird Cage (1996) This film will inspire you to Google the groom's family immediately. Robin Williams plays the owner of the Bird Cage, a Miami nightclub known for its female impersonators, and Nathan Lane plays the club's headliner. They are also the parents of the groom. The parents of the bride are not privy to this information before meeting the groom's family, forcing the father of the bride, Gene Hackman, to borrow both a dress and a wig in order to fit in.

Father of the Bride (1991) This film is an excellent teaching aid to demonstrate that you have not gone overboard on the wedding plans. Warning: My husband saw this movie and immediately wanted to hire their wedding planner Franck.

Father of the Bride (1950) Avoid this

film at all costs: You don't want to know what $5,000 used to buy.

Four Weddings and a Funeral (1994) View this film as a cautionary tale about incompetent officiants, absurd wedding dresses, and inviting guests who look better than the bride.

The In-Laws (1979) (2003) Both the Peter Falk–Alan Arkin original and the Michael Douglas–Albert Brooks remake offer clear examples of how the father of the groom should not behave.

Meet the Parents (2000) Robert DeNiro demonstrates extreme techniques for getting to know a potential son-in-law.

My Best Friend's Wedding (1997) Observe the groom's gorgeous ex-girlfriend. If your daughter's intended has a similar friend, you'll want to make sure that her invitation mysteriously disappears on the way to the post office.

My Big Fat Greek Wedding (2002) This film provides convincing evidence that a good wedding can survive misspelled invitations, ugly bridesmaids' dresses, an ugly wedding dress, and zits.

Monsoon Wedding (2001) The filmmaker demonstrates the universality of problems with wedding vendors and offers helpful advice on dealing with relatives who probably shouldn't have been invited in the first place.

Notting Hill (1999) This film will allay doubts about some destination weddings, illustrating the advantages of an American bride marrying in England. In short, the mother of the bride gets to wear a terrific hat.

Polish Wedding (1998) Although there is no wedding on screen, and the wedding preparation is limited to "motivating" the reluctant groom with a hockey stick, this movie is worth viewing because the mother of the bride is the sexiest person on screen.

Pretty Woman (1990) This film demonstrates that all girls share the same romantic fantasy, even if they grow up to be hookers.

The Runaway Bride (1999) This film provides examples of four different weddings and four distinct wedding styles. Watch this with your daughter—it shows that it isn't the right dress, the right place, or the reception that counts. It's the right groom at the right time.

Steel Magnolias (1989) This is a cinematic primer for creating a Southern wedding. Take note of the big skirts, big picture hats, big hair, and the armadillo groom's cake.

That Old Feeling (1997) Under the astute direction of Carl Reiner, Bette Midler and Dennis Farina demonstrate how parents reenacting their marriage wars can ruin a daughter's wedding.

The Wedding Banquet (1993) (in English and Chinese, with subtitles) An early work by director Ang Lee, this film offers an introduction to Chinese wedding celebrations and an object lesson about parental acceptance of children's choices.

The Wedding Planner (2001) The filmmaker provides an exemplary look at the work of an upscale wedding planner. The film's wedding emergency kit should be studied for possible replication.

The Wedding Singer (1998) After observing this cinematic case study on the perils of employing the wrong musicians, you may reevaluate the advantages of utilizing an electronic alternative.